A SICILIAN'S JOURNEY

William V. Fioravanti

This book is dedicated to my grandfather Guglielmo (William) Fioravanti.

A life without risks is no life at all.

Acknowledgments

In acknowledging the many people who helped contribute to this book, I would like to start with my nephew, Erik Douglass, who provided the impetus for me to write of this journey and my late aunt, Mary Fioravanti Doz who filled me with so many memories. Also, I need to credit the people who helped me jump-start this project. The input and materials offered to me by my cousin, Rosemary Andreana Occhino, the initial material given to me by Nina Candaro Lathers and information by Morris Evans, were invaluable. Credit should also be given to the spiritual and economic support magnanimously given by: Michael and Terry McCarthy, Bruno Hofmann, Roseanne and Jay Kaplan, Ray and Paula Bishop, Steve Pope, and John Inserra. Thanks also must go to: Josie and Bruno DeSantis, Jenny Mrha, Agatha Fioravanti Douglass, John Alfano, Kathy Sullivan, Anna O'Connell, Richard Aulisi, Lucy Izzano, and Thomas Fioravanti.

The most important "thank you" is to Bette Fioravanti who, without her blazing belief and constant pushing and editing of this book, it would have never been completed. She was positive and persistent in her attitude towards me. Thanks!

Preface

Before beginning, the saga of "A Sicilian's Journey", certain aspects must be clarified. It is important to understand that dates mentioned in the story, together with close details and aspects of the characters' lives may be less than accurate. The modes of transportation, descriptions of educational institutions and the characters' abodes may vary from the actual time in question, and Anglo-Saxon names will be employed as the story progresses in order to move it along at a more rapid pace. However, an attempt will be made to minimize these discrepancies as much as possible while the author recalls events to the best of his ability.

Part One

Chapter 1: Crossings

Vincenzo Saviotti gazed across the Straits of Messina and wondered how many times in his life he had made the crossing from Messina to Reggio Calabria. It was November, 1880, and the winds blew cold and stiff around the mountain range and the countryside. Vincenzo shuddered and wiped his running nose. What had happened to so suddenly change his peasant life?

In 1878, in order to increase his earnings, Vincenzo had made a decision to expand his travelling cobbling trade. The small villages, where he plied his trade and which filled the countryside from Sicilian towns and provinces of Castelmola and Messina, were becoming less prosperous and he was finding it much harder to make a living. Thus it was that he made a decision to venture across the Straits of Messina in order to enhance his business. It happened that Vincenzo would change his life completely and start in motion a chain of events that would ultimately lead many people half way across the world.

Vincenzo came from a small Sicilian village called Castelmola which overlooked the beautiful, historic city of Taormina, once believed to be the land of the lotus eaters, as described in Homer's famous epic, "The Odyssey". The city of Taormina also boasted ownership of one of the best still-standing Greek and Roman amphitheaters which gave it a significant prestige in Sicily. The Saviotti family had been in Castelmola for many generations and it is difficult to try to trace its precise genealogy. How Vincenzo had become a cobbler is not clear, but it is known that he would pass down this trade to his children in the years to come.

He married very early and had three children whose names are not known. One of the Saviotti sons had a boy who would eventually go to America and become very affluent.

It came to pass that Vincenzo could not support his family by plying his trade solely in Castelmola so he made what seemed to be a very good business decision to become a travelling cobbler and this was the story's beginning of the Fioravanti and Andreana families.

A ferry which ran daily from San Giovanni to Messina arrived on time at the port and Vincenzo and his burro boarded it to make the journey to Calabria. Arrangements had earlier been made for a very pregnant Maria to meet Vincenzo and to quickly depart on the returning ferry to Messina. Vincenzo and his new love Maria was soon to give birth, in 1881 to a child who would be known as Giuseppe Andreana.

Maria, who was the author's great-grand-mother, was a beautiful fiery red-head who turned many a man's eye. A union was created between Vincenzo and Maria, which would last for the rest of their lives and it was a union that would prove to be not holy, but defiantly not unholy. Vincenzo discovered Maria just outside the port where they had planned to meet and they quickly made their way back to the ferry. Once on board, heading for Sicily and Castelmola, they would never look back.

Chapter 2: The Return

The sun was beginning to illuminate the Calabrian Mountains and there appeared a glow on the water in the Straits of Messina. Vincenzo Saviotti had planned it so that the return journey would be in the sunny day-time hours that would warm Maria and himself. The journey was to take six to seven hours since the roads at present were still very rough and crude.

The distance between the city of Messina and the town of Taormina was some thirty miles and the journey then continued for a mile and a half up a dangerously challenging mountain-path which led to the village of Castelmola. Prior to the trip, Vincenzo Saviotti had secured a wagon, or as was more commonly called a Sicilian cart. Here in this land, the carts were as much cherished as cars would later be and they were so well-revered that they were crafted into miniature forms with glorious colored embellishments and their little horses and are still sold even today to tourists in every Sicilian marketplace. It can be noted that Alfio, in what is the most famous Sicilian opera,"Cavelleria Rusticana", and in what is a substantiation of this information, brings his cart and burro onstage in most theatrical productions.

Maria was bundled up against the cold to protect her and the unborn child. When all had been in place, they had begun their journey. Vincenzo had had ample time to contemplate all that had transpired since that very first day when he saw the fiery red tresses and lost his head and his heart. He suspected that, even if he had been a free single man, it would have been just as difficult to win such a beauty since he was a good ten years Maria's senior, and he felt inadequate when first he touched her. However, as fate would have it, from that very first day she was smitten by him. They began a romance which eventually had led to this present situation. When Maria announced that she was pregnant, Vincenzo Saviotti showed a resolve which would be his mark forever.

The Raneri family in Castelmola was close friends to Vincenzo, and he wasted no time in securing with them a room in their house for Maria and himself which was just a block away from where he had previously lived with his wife and their three children. He had decided to stay close to his legitimate family, but he would not relinquish the love of his life. Believing this to be truly material for an opera, Vincenzo, like most Sicilians echoed, a lust and spirit for life which started in his heart and, only after plunging headlong into the eternal fire of love did he begin to think with his head. By then it was too late.

Vincenzo Saviotti stopped half way through the journey to feed Maria, rest the burro, and to have a glass of wine for himself. He assured her, as she was very nervous at the prospect of encountering Vincenzo's first family, that all would be fine and that he would always be at her side. She was comforted by this and, at the moment, realized that she would always be able to count on Vincenzo's strength.

The rest of the trip was fairly uneventful and they finally arrived in Taormina. As they stopped at the beginning of the upwards path which led to the hill of Castelmola, Vincenzo heaved a sigh of relief as he gazed at Maria, and commenced the final mile and a half of the journey.

Chapter 3: The Arrival

Upon their arrival at Castelmola, the stage was set for a typical Sicilian melodrama. As Vincenzo and Maria stepped into the piazza, there appeared several people who were supposedly leisurely talking and smoking. The burro, which had been carrying Maria, was anything but inconspicuous. It was as if a whistle had gone off. In the distance could be heard a shrill cry of,"Puttana, puttana", which in translation means "The whore is here". Vincenzo's wife was infuriating and terrifying as she kept on screaming.

This was not a time for one in Vincenzo's position to falter and lose control of the situation. He grabbed Maria's hand, took hold of the burro, and headed for the room at the Raneri's which would become his sanctuary for the next few years. The Castelmola residents looked on as the newest citizen was led to her new home.

Maria wondered how her lover would be able to provide for so many with so little at his disposal. She would soon realize that Vincenzo would find a way for all of them to survive and that he would later teach his skills to the children.

All families in Castelmola had access to land on the mountain-sides where they farmed as, what were called contour farmers, in order to survive. They became known to the world as "contandini" and were considered to be the poorest people in the western world. By the early 1900's, these contandini would be the primary export of both Italy and Sicily to America.

The couple reached the small room in the Raneri house and felt safe for the first time in a few days. Vincenzo comforted Maria and assured her of the future. She looked about her and, even though she was impoverished, a strange feeling of hope seemed to fill both the room and herself. The baby was beginning to move inside her and this new life became a blessing to this woman in this strange place.

As day turned to night and all the gossip, yelling and conjecture subsided, a peace settled over Castelmola. All was right with the world again, and the local inhabitants of this small mountain village would have much to talk about in the days and months to come. However, Vincenzo Saviotti would teach those peasants how to coexist in a world alien to most Sicilians and to most Italians. The volcano of Mount Etna started to smoke in the distance. This was, perhaps, signaling that turmoil, in the land of perpetual turmoil, had now been quelled.

Chapter 4: Peaceful Co-Existence

Time flew by for Maria and months passed quicker than she could have imagined. The year was 1881 and, with the help of a midwife, Maria easily gave birth to a healthy boy whom Vincenzo and Maria were to name Giuseppe. Unfortunately, since the child was born out of wedlock, the Taormina city officials followed the Italian Government's ruling of choosing the surname, and he was given that of Giuseppe Andreana, and not that of his real father, Saviotti. The boy, however, was a joy to his parents, and as Vincenzo had promised, Maria found that she could survive and find a new life among these strange island people.

Maria's day to day life became a daily routine between her care for her child and her work on the mountain where she grew most of the food that would be for meals to share with the baby and Vincenzo. The small piece of land which she farmed was graciously given to Vincenzo by his oldest and trusted friend, Peppino Raneri.

In the late nineteenth century, Castelmola was not the beautiful village that it would become in the years after World War 11. It was a poor, small village of about two hundred and fifty people who lived in what can be easily described as adobe huts. Most of these homes only had one room whose sections were separated by sheets of various fabrics hanging from the ceiling. These adobe huts were dull, dreary and depressing. There were no fireplaces and most heat came from what resembled hearths which were also used for cooking.

So where was the beauty that Maria found in this impoverished village? The beauty that persevered and transcended, war, and the ravages of weather was from the beautiful vistas which existed at every viewpoint. From the piazza could be seen Isla Bella, Taormina and Mazzaro Beach. Looking south from the piazza could be seen Mount Etna, in all its majesty, billowing smoke in the distance as if she were a great ruler reminding all in its boundaries to tread carefully. This was the divine beauty of Castelmola which would carry all of her poor inhabitants into the future.

Sicilians are strange people and, as they grew to finally embrace Maria and her child, she found a love for all those whom she encountered in the village. Vincenzo's first Saviotti family came to know and care for his new family. These were the beginnings of what were to be the Andreana and soon-to-be Fioravanti legacies.

Chapter 5: It Starts

Thunder and lightning split the air, and Mount Etna was spewing fire like a giant furnace. It was as if the Greeks had left all their gods behind when they fled the island some centuries ago and were now awakened to wreak havoc and instill fear in the poor Castelmola inhabitants.

Maria Testa, which was her maiden name, was giving birth to another son and she could hardly pay attention to all that was going on outside the small quarters where she lived. Her first son, Giuseppe Andreana, was playing on the floor, wrapped in a cotton sweater. For a Sicilian January it was colder than usual and this climate change caused extra suffering to these poor natives.

Vincenzo stood by as he watched the midwife deliver a frail yet handsome baby boy to Maria's arms. It was January 20, 1884, and the beginning of the Guglielmo-Fioravanti family. To be sure, Vincenzo had no idea at this time that his second son would be given a different name from the first.

Since the weather had been finally reduced to calm, Vincenzo travelled down the mountain to Taormina to go to the Municipal Office, and he was thinking about how he had been able to successfully support two families. The oldest Saviotti son had by now established himself as a permanent cobbler in Taormina and was doing fairly well. He had been a great asset to Vincenzo in helping to provide for the two families. Somehow, some way, all had been able to thrive in this impoverished environment.

Vincenzo was feeling a surge of pride as he entered the Municipal Building and approached the nearby clerk to whom he gave the required new-birth information. Looking in the great book, the clerk finally spoke and wrote down the name: Guglielmo Fioravanti. Vincenzo was then handed a document stating the baby's birthday and the new name and was aware, however, that the illegitimate children would never have his name, but he had thought that the new sons would both carry the same surname. This would not be the case and they would from now on be brothers in blood but never brothers in name.

Yes. The gods had awakened and soon they would enjoy playing with the lives of Giuseppe and Guglielmo. The two brothers would live to have adventures that, for the time and the conditions, would take great courage.

Things had changed in both Italy and Sicily. Italy had become unified and the Risorgimento had had a monumental effect on the people of Sicily which now had an expanded train and transportation system. Roads were better and general education was coming to all people of both countries. It was education that would be the catalyst to propel the Andreana and Fioravanti families into the twentieth century.

Chapter 6: Growing Up

If the Gods had truly awakened, it was not just to torment the people of Castelmola. In some strange fashion, from the birth of Guglielmo through the next fifteen years, despair would haunt the people of both Italy and Sicily. From 1884 to 1887, the great cholera epidemic would ravage all of Italy and most of Sicily. Death tolls during this period were devastating, but Guglielmo and Giuseppe survived. Poverty was at an all-time high for both Italy and Sicily, yet brothers, their families and many inhabitants of Castelmola survived. The worst economic conditions and illiteracy since before the unification existed and yet Guglielmo and Giuseppe learned to not only read and write rudimentary Italian, but to become completely literate and they were well educated for the time. As for nourishment, farming on the side of the mountain together with what Vincenzo garnered for payment from his trade, provided for their well-being.

The two boys grew and learned that in many ways their lot was not as hopeless as it would appear to outsiders. They were loved by their father and mother and embraced by their half-brothers and half-sisters. This environment gave them the esteem which they needed to blossom into strong-minded and intelligent young men.

As for Taormina, it was their salvation since it boasted one of the best "proper" schools in the area and citizens of Castelmola were allowed to attend as regular students along with the other children of Taormina. Due to the fact that 84% of the Italian and Sicilian people were illiterate, what Vincenzo allowed his boys to do was indeed unprecedented at the time.

Guglielmo and Giuseppe would travel down the mountain each day on foot to reach the school. Vincenzo would allow the boys to take the burro when he found that he did not need to use it himself. This would make it so much easier for two young boys to deal with the difficult journey. Giuseppe liked school but Guglielmo found that he really had a very strong passion for it and soon became an avid reader. He had an extremely inquisitive mind and was hungry for knowledge. His education would serve him well in his early childhood in Sicily.

As time passed, there appeared another family which would have a big impact on the two boys. This Valentino family, as they were named, became Guglielmo's main obsession. He would fall in love with one of the daughters and would learn his first lesson of heartbreak.

There were two brothers in the Valentino family of whom the second had one son and one daughter. This son would eventually become a vile and nefarious person who would hurt many people in both Sicily and in America.

Vincenzo's second family moved from the Raneri quarters to a place owned by the Dallora's. They now had two rooms, which was an improvement from their first living quarters, and the boys were able to study and read in comparative peace.

Guglielmo trained to be a cobbler alongside his studies, but Giuseppe had absolutely no interest in his father's trade and eventually would leave home and work in Messina as a book-binder. It was during this time that there was much strife and turmoil in Sicily which was about to lose its biggest industry, sulfur mining. At this time, Texas had recently discovered its own plentiful supply of sulfur and was no longer in need of this Sicilian export. Italy's economy was also greatly affected from this since it too was a financial beneficiary of the Sicilian mines.

Yes. The Gods seemed to protect the Sicilians but, at the same time, torment them. Could it get worse?

Chapter 7: Young Love

Is young love for the very poor the same as it is for the more educated, affluent members of society? It is not the author's intention to turn this story into a Sicilian "Portnoy's Complaint", but those with nothing and who know virtually nothing, may be very inclined to act prematurely on basic primeval instincts. Perhaps for the poor it is experienced on a baser level! Males and females of the lower classes reach an age when they start to awaken to feelings and impulses that eventually lead to a mature form of lovemaking. Our heroes are not of this ilk since they had the advantage of a literate education. Guglielmo and Giuseppe had explored the wonders of Dante, Cicero, and of the father of Italian realism (Verismo), Giovanni Verga, who was responsible for the two famous Sicilian novels, "La Lupa" and "Cavalleria Rusticana," the last of which became adapted into a well-known one-act opera.

It would be fair to state that Giuseppe and Guglielmo, while growing up, were devoid of toys and other articles that would make young boys elated and proud. They had to play with their father's cobbling lasts for amusement and, at times, other items such as a broken cart or an old wheel which their father may have received for payment of his work.

The two boys had supplemented their play with education that they gained in Taormina. When they were in their early teens they would go down the mountain, watch operas, and listen to music and see the travelling troubadours who performed at the Teatro Greco-Romano Amphitheatre. It could be said that, in spite of the poverty and illiteracy that plagued most of Sicily and Italy at this time, these two boys had acquired a certain culture not found in many poor homes during this period.

As the boys were growing up, they were constantly aware that the Valentino girls did not live very far away. Now that Guglielmo had reached the age of fifteen, he was feeling the fires of puberty and, as it would happen, those feelings were directed at Rosalia, one of the four Valentino daughters.

The Valentino family was very poor and the parents, Carmine and Sara, found themselves struggling to support the girls whose names were Agata, Lucia, Caterina and Rosalia, and Carmine, the father, was hard-pressed to support his daughters and was readily willing to relinquish any one of them if it alleviated his struggle. In time, he would have this dream come true.

Now Giuseppe, about to turn eighteen, had become quite a Lothario in Castelmola, but he never settled on any particular girl. He had his own dream of leaving this small confining village to explore the wonders of a large city and he chose Messina as his destination. After discussing his decision with his parents, he said goodbye to them and to his brother, and was on his way.

By this time, Guglielmo had become very close to Rosalia and he came to think of her exclusively, and she felt the same way about him. She was a lovely girl with light brown hair and deep, dark eyes. It was those eyes which had made Guglielmo fall madly in love with her and which he pictured constantly. Rosalia's one sister, Agata, although older, had herself fallen for Guglielmo. This was her secret to be kept in her heart but which was to give her much grief in the future.

Agata, not being as pretty as her sister, Rosalia, had a strength and resolve which was akin to that of Vincenzo. Her stature was short and stocky, and she was fiercely loyal to her friends and family. This little Sicilian woman would have no problem surviving later in the new world.

In time, Rosalia and Guglielmo would become engaged and it appeared to all that it was a union created by the Gods. Nevertheless, from the distance, there loomed a force that would alter the lives of all those connected with this Sicilian melodrama. This force was none other than Salvatore Valentino, Carmine Valentino's nephew. The furies would once again raise their ugly heads!

Chapter 8: Sulfur and Conscription

Guglielmo Fioravanti and Salvatore Valentino's lives would suddenly turn in completely different directions. When Salvatore reached the age of sixteen, his father sold him into slavery to the sulfur mine owners. In return for handing over his son, Salvatore's father received a small amount of money, which was something like twenty dollars. This payment was considered a loan, but was never paid back. In the mines of Enna, where the long thin sulfur veins followed a line as far as Mount Etna, miners slaved there side by side with boys as young as six years old. Sicilians came to know the harsh price to be paid in a life of bondage. Once again, the awful exploitation of the workers by the aristocracy became a driving force which propelled so many Sicilians to the New World. Salvatore Valentino continued to toil in the mines for the next few years and when he ultimately left, it would be with a vengeance.

Italy did not have its own sulfur at this time, but did receive revenue from the Sicilian mines and was important to both economies. It was sulfur, commonly called Sicilian Gold, which gave the impetus to thrust Italy into the industrial Revolution, and Sicily followed closely behind and was the largest sulfur producer in the world at this time.

Life in Castelmola was getting more difficult by the day as poverty was at an all-time high. Vincenzo Saviotti could not pursue his cobbling trade as his health was slipping away and Guglielmo, his son, was frustrated by making little or no money. His only joy was his relationship with Rosalia. He knew that something must change lest all the family would perish from hunger or eventually disease.

Sicily's great sulfur production had placed an extra burden on the young men at this time of war and they were now needed for the Italian army. For many years, Italy had engaged itself in conscription and was now desperate for recruits. Guglielmo made a decision to enlist, and he approached Rosalia to explain his reasons for this. He would gain financial benefits and this would be far superior to trying to make attempts at survival in Castelmola. Rosalia was sympathetic to Guglielmo's reasoning and wished him well. The two kissed after they had decided there and then to become engaged. Rosalia told her family of this happy event and all were extremely positive except for Agata who suffered greatly from this news.

As Guglielmo said his good-byes to his parents, in another part of Sicily Salvatore was planning to escape from the bondage of the sulfur mines. He had learned many things about sulfur. All the miners were trained as to how to prevent sulfur, which is extremely flammable, from igniting. The required lessons on fire-prevention methods also exposed the means by which sulfur fires could be started, and Salvatore would later make use of this knowledge. He was responsible for setting the fuse that would turn the whole mine into a blazing inferno and thus made a passage for his freedom. He had worked out his plans to leave the island, go to the port of Naples, and then sail to America where money had already been put aside there for him by his boyhood friend, Tony Cundaro. Salvatore's plan of escape went well and, as the mine exploded, he made his escape and was on his way to the New World.

Guglielmo's life, on the other hand, was equally exciting. He, as a soldier, was stationed in Messina and, with his ability to read and write, was promoted to corporal and assigned as an assistant to a Captain DePasquale. This new posting for Guglielmo would serve to introduce him to new vistas and further expand his horizons.

Chapter 9: Life and Death

The now Corporal Guglielmo Fioravanti gazed into the mirror and wondered whose countenance was reflecting back at him. He hardly recognized the fuller face with its finely trimmed moustache that was now decorating his upper lip. He could see the top of his closely-fitted dark grey uniform that bore a collar which wound around his neck like a leg-iron.

Guglielmo's quarters in Messina were by no means extravagant but far superior to what he had been accustomed to in his native Castelmola. His was a life to be envied by many and, he owed it all to the Captain.

Captain Depasquale was an aristocrat from Giardina, a town on the outskirts of Taormina. The men in his family had been in the military for generations and he was following the tradition. Later, however, his own son broke the custom and became a prominent surgeon. The Captain had taken an immediate liking to Guglielmo and promptly promoted him to Corporal, making him his personal aide. What wonderful worlds now opened up to Guglielmo under the Captain's tutelage! Opera now became a focal point in Guglielmos' life. Together they travelled to Milan and visited La Scala, which at the time was the greatest opera house of the day. In Rome he discovered the works of Leonardo DaVinci, Michelangelo and the Coliseum building all of which created wonder to the man who was no more than a boy at heart. A world of philosophy now appeared to him in the form of books written by the great nineteenth century leaders of Italy and Sicily. Names such as Mazzini, Giraboldi and Cavour, known to generations as the fire, the sword, and the heart, became well-known to Guglielmo and their works and ideas filled his mind and thoughts.

One night, Guglielmo was preparing to meet his brother, Giuseppe, for an evening of dining and conversation. The two brothers had not seen each other often enough in recent years and both felt excitement at the chance of spending time together. They met at a very nice restaurant near the Straits of Messina and enjoyed together several glasses of wine. During the evening there was much conversation particularly about Vincenzo and Maria and of their sick parents in Castelmola about whom they were constantly awaiting bad news.

After the mine explosion which preceded his escape, life had been hard for Salvatore Valentino. He landed on Ellis Island in New York on May 11, 1903, that by now had become known to immigrants as the "Island of Tears," and found his boyhood friend, Tony Cundaro, waiting for him. After greeting each other warmly, they departed for Johnstown, a small town in the foothills of the Adirondack Mountains. Tony Cundaro had made a living working on the railroad which followed both the Mohawk and Hudson Rivers. When Tony reached Fonda, he followed the new spur that wound its way from there to Johnstown. Liking the looks of this small town, he decided to plant his roots and settle since he had heard that Johnstown was badly in need of good carpenters and building laborers for which he might be found readily qualified. Tony had skills and ability and Salvatore had brute strength which came from his being his six feet tall and cast him as quite a strong, imposing figure. Since the mines, life had not been easy for Salvatore but, compared to the sulfur mines, it was much better and he now believed that he would escape the possibility of dying young or of being crippled for life. He sometimes thought that all his present toil and sweat were nothing compared to what he may have endured had he stayed in Sicily.

When three years in America had passed by for Salvatore, he had saved a substantial amount of money which he planned to use on a return trip back to Sicily on unfinished business. Some his friends back there had assured him that he was not a suspect in the mine explosion, but he was not totally convinced of this and would later wreak havoc on some of his old enemies. Salvatore had a unique ability to cause pain and suffering and these two talents would soon become a part of his way of life.

It was a blazingly hot day, in 1905, and Vincenzo was making his way up the mountain trail to Castelmola. Of late, he had been experiencing sharp chest pains and on this particular day, the pains he felt were very severe. Gasping for breath, he fell to his knees and seemed to die an immediate death as his heart gave out. His days on earth now ended, all Vincenzo left behind to the world were his beloved Maria and their children.

In the meantime, Guglielmo and Giuseppe finished their evening together in Messina, and little did they know that the very next day they would learn of their father's sudden passing. From the sudden death of their father, the two boys became men overnight. Death certainly has a way of doing this.

Chapter 10: Homecoming

In 1906, Guglielmo was in his final tour of military duty. After the next seven months, he would be back permanently in Castelmola. As much as he had enjoyed and benefitted from all that he had learned while in the army, he still felt a yearning for his little old mountainside home. He yearned for Rosalia and the sight of Mount Etna smoking in the distance. In later years, all the Fioravanti members would be cursed by that same smoldering desire to return to their home town. Even the sometimes violent and dramatic family arguments could not diminish family bonds. Time and again and forever, they would want to return to their roots.

As Guglielmo dreamed of his return, somewhere across the ocean, another dreamed of his return to Castelmola. Salvatore Valentino had always had such deep burning desires for his cousin Rosalia whom he considered was rightfully his, and not Guglielmo's. Since he did not yet have to support a wife and a family, he saved most of the monies earned from his laboring, and could return to Sicily with ample funds. In making the travel plans, he still had reservations that he was thought guilty by some with respects to the mine explosion. However, he would deal with that when he arrived. His first goal was to secure the hand of Rosalia and when he arrived back at Castelmola in January, 1906, with his pockets stuffed with money, he made his way to his Uncle Carmine's house to make him an offer about marrying his cousin. If Carmine would secure his cousin's hand in marriage, then he would receive a substantial amount of money. Being reluctant at first, eventually Carmine agreed and the condition was made that Rosalia would return to America with Salvatore. After all was settled, the two were married shortly thereafter.

Rosalia was overwhelmed by this sudden turn of events in her poor mundane life. As much as she thought she loved Guglielmo, she was intoxicated with the idea of seeing new places and experiencing thoughts of exciting adventure. In many ways, she was correct in her flights of fantasy. Her life would be full of adventure but not in the way she had imagined. She was about to experience a life of pain and disappointment. Salvatore's life, in sharp contrast, would have him live up to the reputation he had acquired working down the mines. He would set the world on fire!

After their marriage, Salvatore and Rosalia left Castelmola to go to another small Sicilian town called Belmonte. Salvatore had secured a small dwelling there and contemplated his future plans. He wasted no time in deciding upon his course of action. By the middle of May, 1906, he sent Rosalia on a ship from Palermo, bound for New York. She arrived at the end of May and was met at the New York docks by Tony Cundaro. She was only twenty-one and was much too innocent to suspect that she would now be embarking on a future life of terror and despair.

Agata Valentino was one figure in this melodrama that was still optimistic about her future, and she envisioned for herself a more perfect plan than the one which Salvatore had had in mind for Rosalia. The way had been made clear now for Agata to capture the heart of Guglielmo Fioravanti and, hopefully, have her dream of love come true.

Maria, who rarely saw her sons now, had been trying to reach Guglielmo to tell him of the tragic events that would certainly send him into a deep depression. Now she felt even herself to be tormented in her loneliness by all that had happened since her husband's untimely death.

Both Italian and Sicilian trains have long had a reputation for unpunctuality. It would later take the fascist dictator, Mussolini, to fix this. So it was that Guglielmo's train would, according to habit, arrive late in Taormina and there was subsequently no-one to meet him. Evening was upon him as he rushed to make his way up the mountain to Castelmola, and he was filled with anticipation at the thought of seeing his mother and future bride. Soon his bubble would burst as he approached the piazza and met his crying mother. She would relate to him all of the recent events which would forever change the course of his life. He had certainly become a man now and was extremely handsome and dashing in his military uniform and highly polished boots.

Now, with the arrival of her son, Maria did not feel completely alone that night in the piazza, and noticed Agata sitting by the fountain. She, after her long patient wait, would soon be able to have her say with the man she so dearly loved and whom she would love for many years to come.

Chapter 11: Lost and Found

Feeling lost and in a constant state of despondency and despair, Guglielmo wandered, as if in a drunken state, through the streets of Taormina and Castelmola. Settling back into life in his home town, he tried to work at his cobbling trade, but he had come to loathe mending shoes. The year slipped by at a rapid pace, and he found some solace in his mother's love and was happy to learn of his brother's marriage to a girl from a village outside the city of Palermo. This new sister-in-law was named Josephine and as a new wife would make many visits to Guglielmo and Maria. Time may not allow one to completely forget pain, but it does serve to ease it. Realization that losing something very special is never easy, but there comes a time when the inevitable has to be accepted. Destiny will have its way!

Agata Valentino waited for time to pass and then casually began to find ways of seemingly accidentally running into Guglielmo. She would always initiate conversation with this sad looking man of the mountain village. Before he could understand what was happening, Guglielmo had found that a very strong affection and trust were growing between him and this strong, loyal woman. Suddenly, a light seemed to spark and somehow in his mind, he rationalized that Agata was who he needed to give him the strength to continue.

The marriage between Guglielmo Fioravanti and Agata Valentino took place at the church in Castelmola which stood at the side of the piazza. It was 1908, and for the first time in two years, Guglielmo found a sort of living peace. He renewed his cobbling trade and attempted to carve out a living for his new wife and himself. Their family began to grow as on May 14, 1909, Agata gave birth to a daughter, Maria Mafalda who was named after Guglielmo's mother and in1910, another daughter, Josephine would be born. Maria was healthy and strong and she would in later years be the significant Fioravanti family member to closely chronicle all the major family events. Josephine, the younger daughter, would later die in America at an early age of thirty-three.

News of Salvatore Valentino was sketchy after he left for America, but it was documented that he sailed from Naples in April, 1908 and safely made the crossing to New York. Rosalia, now his wife, had been living in America with Salvatore's friend, Tony Cundaro, and for two years provided for her and now made ready a permanent place for her and her newly arriving husband.

Although Guglielmo was beginning to feel more happy and content with Agata and his new daughter, he still had questions about their future. He asked Captain DePasquale, who agreed, to be godfather to his new child and from this time on, remained a faithful and trusted counselor and friend to both Guglielmo and to Maria as the child grew up.

News from America was very bleak during the first decade of the twentieth century. So many Italians and Sicilians had the notion that, if they were to emigrate to the southern part of America where the climate was similar to that of their own countries, they could avoid experiencing the cold harsh winters which they did not relish. Their evaluation of the prospective bitter weather was correct, but they had no idea of the attitudes which southern Americans would have towards these new immigrants. As it turned out, southern hatred caused hundreds of Italian and, even more Sicilians to be murdered, hung, and burned out of their homes. The southern so-called aristocracy viewed these new immigrants as invaders, working-place scabs, and with a far too liberal tolerance for black people. As luck would have it, the author's family and others who came from the same part of Sicily, were blessed by their choice to relocate to the northern New York State.

Time was running out for mass numbers of immigration to America as quotas were being limited, and Guglielmo knew that he would have to be fast in making this serious decision as to whether or not to immigrate to America. He would make his mind up and this step would prove to be a very harrowing experience.

Chapter 12: The Ultimate Decision

Guglielmo rose from a sleepless night, quietly began to wash, and pack his few meager belongings making ready for what would prove to be the most difficult journey of his life. Moving softly so as to not awaken his wife and daughter, he opened a drawer and Agata stirred from her sleep. He was forced to tell her of his plan and, of course, her first instinct was to attempt to dissuade him not to go. He explained to her of the better life which he was searching for them all and of how dreams could never come true in Sicily but which could certainly become a reality in America. Agata, as a caring wife, was very concerned for Guglielmo's safety, but he tried to convey to her the dangerous situations which were now rising up in their country. Having reassured his wife, he kissed her and the children, Maria and Josephine, and left their house with a small roll of belongings over his shoulder and a small valise which contained most of his cobbling tools. Should the worst case scenario arise, he felt he would be ready to survive through his trade. As he opened the door, the sun was just rising and he started the descent from the top of his mountain sanctuary, for what would be the last climb down for many years to come.

Most of Guglielmo's decisions to take action had begun when his mother died in 1909 and when there were constant rumors of a rising fascist movement, steadily taking over both Italy and Sicily. His wife's family in America was constantly expressing how wonderful life was there and particularly for Agata's sister, Rosalia, and the husband, Salvatore. Guglielmo had constant memories of his army days which had given him courage and now he wondered if he could replicate this courage in his new venture. Believing that he would have the necessary fortitude to survive and show this strength to his American relatives, Rosalia and Salvatore, he had been saving enough money for a passage, earned from his trade.

It was August, 1910, and Guglielmo booked a passage on the Roma ship and promised that he would send for Agata and Maria as soon as he had saved enough money to pay for their tickets and a living place for them all. Agata, with her respect for him, trusted and believed in Guglielmo's words since she knew him as dependable and hard-working. Up to this point in time, he had never let her down and she was sure that his promise of their all being together in America would definitely come to fruition.

Guglielmo made his way to the railway station and boarded the train for Palermo where he would take the Roma Ship, bound for America. The trip was hot and humid, and by the time he reached the docks, he was drenched in sweat since the last weeks of August are so hot in Sicily that temperatures can easily reach 104 degrees. Feeling completely burned up and exhausted, Guglielmo arrived in Palermo and still had to find his way to the port.

The streets of Palermo were crowded and, as he continued on towards the docks, he felt a sensation of being watched. Crossing into an alley, he was pushed by two men who attempted to rob him of what little he had. This meager amount of money was like a matter of life and death to the man who had plans for a long, tumultuous journey. Without these means, he might easily starve to death in this unfamiliar city. With the future now looking very bleak for Guglielmo, suddenly and seemingly out of nowhere, a huge figure burst into the alley and knocked down one of the assailants and proceeded to take away a knife from the one attacker. The man, who had just saved a life, was cut and bleeding as the assailants fled. In his gratitude, Guglielmo unrolled his paltry belongings to take out a white shirt which he was saving for the future, ripped it to make a bandage, and cleaned and dressed his savior's wounds.

This man, who had brought Guglielmo out of a horrifying situation, introduced himself as Giuseppe Brunetto from Graniti and who happened to be sailing himself that very same day on the SS Roma, bound for America. Unlike Guglielmo, Giuseppe was uncertain as to where he would stay upon his arrival since he did not have any relatives over there. Guglielmo told him that he had heard of the seeming opportunities in a town called Johnstown and invited Giuseppe to join him. After they agreed on travelling together, they began what was to be a bonding between men which would last two future generations.

Chapter 13: The Long Voyage and the Island of Tears

It was August 30, 1910 when Guglielmo Fioravanti and his new friend, Giuseppe Brunetto, made their way towards the ship, the SS Roma. When it was time to approach the vessel, they found it to be swarming with Italian Carbinari, the police officers. Giuseppe feared that they were searching for him in connection with the alley altercation earlier that day. However, Guglielmo assured his new friend that was highly unlikely to be the case and they proceeded up the gangway and onto the ship. Before boarding, Guglielmo handed Giuseppe a Sicilian cap for which he indicated his appreciation. It would be the Sicilian cap which became the trademark for all Sicilian immigrants to the New World.

When aboard, the two men had their papers cleared and were directed to the steerage area where most of the poorer passengers, who had paid approximately $35 for the journey and numbered some one thousand, four hundred and fifty-four, were assigned. On this trip, there were only fifty-four first-class passengers who had paid the higher price of about $75.

As the ship set off, Guglielmo tried to recall memories of his life during the time he had spent in Sicily and in Italy. The first senses that came into his mind were those of sadness and the loss of all dear to him. He had doubts as to whether or not he would be able to find the strength to cope with not being able to see his wife and daughters and, on a daily basis, suffered the most worrisome thoughts of facing his ex-love, Rosalia and her husband, Salvatore. At his weakest moment, his wonderings were interrupted by Giuseppe Brunetto who too expressed fears of anticipation at the thought of facing life anew in America.

Giuseppe's biggest fear was not being able to make himself an indispensable asset to an American company in the New World. He had no particular trade or skills to offer. On the other hand, Guglielmo had his cobbling skills to lean on

and he comforted Giuseppe by asserting that he had heard that
there were a lot of companies who would give work to laborers
prepared to work for twelve to fourteen hours a day. This was
true as in Johnstown and, in its neighboring town of
Gloversville, the leather-tanning and glove-making businesses
were now starting to flourish at a rapid pace. Leather-tanning
in New York State had been carried out for many years by the
native Indians of the area, due to the large population of deer,
but making leather gloves was completely new. After this
information given to him by his friend, Giuseppe felt less
anxious and more comforted and settled down for the rest of
the journey.

They had been sailing for three days after leaving
Palermo, and all the steerage passengers, for this is where all
immigrants were, had awful claustrophobia and felt overcome
with the stale body stench and the lack of fresh air at the
bottom part of the ship. Food given to the steerage passengers
consisted of various soups and slices of stale bread which were
as base and frugal as could be without causing dysentery and
disease. It was during the journey that Guglielmo, a very
personable fellow, made the acquaintance of one of the night-
shift-stewards. He patrolled the deck to make sure that the
steerage passengers stayed in their allotted places and, on
becoming friendly with Guglielmo, allowed him and Giuseppe
to sneak above board during the evening when the other
passengers were distracted, and breathe some fresh air and
escape the filthy odors. This act of kindness certainly helped
them to retain their sanity.

The SS Roma sailed into New York and it passed by the
Statue of Liberty bearing its famous inscription concerning the
poor, the hungry and the unwanted and headed for Ellis Island.
It would be later that Italians and Sicilians would call this
island, "The Island of Tears", as it had a paradoxical meaning
for so many who stepped onto it. Some anticipated hopes and
desires for a much better life than they ever could have attained
in the old world back home, but the other unfortunate side of

the coin was that, should the immigrants want to return to their native land, it would be virtually impossible and the attempt would be a dreadful ordeal.

Guglielmo was very fortunate in that he spoke some English and had little trouble going through the many examinations and tests which all the immigrants had to endure before receiving a stamp which said, "You may enter through these gates and step into America." Feeling a terrible sense of loneliness at this point, Guglielmo had thoughts of suicide but overcame this negativity and summoned strength to move forward. Having overcome the tedium of this terrible ordeal through customs, he walked onto American soil and suddenly knew that he had come to the land where he would spend the rest of his days. With a sudden rush of elation that now filled his whole body, all he had to do was to wait for his friend, Joe Brunetto, to step onto American soil and they would be on their way to Johnstown, New York.

Chapter 14: Grand Central Station and the Train Ride

On September 8, 1910, having finally cleared the examinations of Ellis Island, the two friends headed for the ferry which would take them to Manhattan. The very thought of what lay ahead made Guglielmo's head swim with anticipation, doubts, and with the thrill of his life's new adventure. He relayed many of his thoughts to Giuseppe who, himself, was also feeling a sense of elation. He shared his ideas and first impressions of the New World with Giuseppe and what this could mean to people such as them. Giuseppe felt himself suddenly to have developed a native intelligence he had not felt before. He saw America as a big country and uttered his belief and trust that they could be big themselves in this enormous country. Guglielmo was aware, however, that they would need to be careful as strangers in a new land where they had much to learn. On this point he had a clarity which in later years would prove him right.

Finally, the ferry landed and the two newest citizens of the United States stepped out into the New World. Feeling yet again elation and expectancy, they set off to find Grand Central Station which would put them on their way to Upstate New York and eventually to Johnstown.

At this time, Grand Central Station, was soon to be replaced by a new permanent one which would take four years to build and which was temporarily located on the east side of New York between Forty-Second and Forty-Third Streets. Guglielmo and Giuseppe found the old station without difficulty. Its edifice was overpowering and grand and was a sight to make these two peasant boys gaze in wonderment. They secured their train tickets for the arduous journey whose route followed the lay of the land alongside the Hudson and Mohawk Rivers. It had been the wonder of engineering and the stupendous natural beauty of the landscape which had inspired such a feat of construction. Guglielmo and Giuseppe could not fail to notice how much more luxurious the train was compared to the rustic, wooden-seated trains back home. For what seemed like the first time since leaving Sicily, the two men fell into a restful, peaceful sleep.

There were five families in total who would come to Johnstown after having left their village of Castelmola. They were: the Raneri's, the Cundaro's, the Valentino's, the Dallora's and the protagonists of this story, the Fioravanti's together with their half siblings, the Andreana's. Giuseppe Andreana did make it to Johnstown but was called to serve in the Italian army and was subsequently killed. After Giuseppe Andreana's death, his wife found the loneliness of her loss together with the harsh winters much too hard to bear and she moved her family back to Sicily. The son, whom she had borne while she lived in America, would return in later years to make his life in Johnstown and Gloversville. His return would now increase the number of Castelmolan immigrant families to six. It is a strange phenomenon that all these six families, who had originated from the same Sicilian village, never formed any close bond between them, yet it would be the off-springs of these six families who later formed close ties to each other in their struggle together against the powerful bigotry which they encountered in schools, stores, and the workplace. Their outward appearance was different from most Johnstown inhabitants with their generally curly hair and complexions that were dark and swarthy. They could, on the whole, speak very little English, and this created a big communication problem and caused a lack of self-confidence and feelings of low self-esteem. They were even reluctant to use their own Sicilian Christian names since they thought that they would be further ostracized. Names such as Giuseppe and Salvatore were Anglicized to Joseph and Sam. Even the Slovak immigrants seemed to be a much better fit than the Sicilians.

As the train journey was coming to a close, William and Joseph disembarked and caught a trolley which would bring them to Johnstown. By now, William was beginning to feel a dark foreboding about his first encounter with his ex-fiancée and Salvatore, now called Sam. There was only a glimmer of happiness while reflecting upon the very hard journey which they had struggled to survive. Now they would have to ready themselves to survive against other hard struggles ahead.

Chapter 15: Johnstown and Gloversville

Italians, like many ethnic groups, are very clannish, and for some reason, Sicilians settled in Johnstown and Neapolitans from Naples, Italy, settled in nearby Gloversville. It was very unusual to find a Neapolitan living in Johnstown or vice versa. Primary concern in this saga is with those who settled in Johnstown, New York.

Johnstown was divided into the four geographic parts: north, south, east and west. The wealthy of the community lived in the southern part of the town. People who inhabited this section of Johnstown were primarily Anglo-Saxon Protestants, and this group was made up of merchants, bankers and factory owners. Many lived on the streets called William and South Perry, which were very elegant in their day.

The eastern part of the city was mostly Irish and had the most beautiful Catholic Church which was, in fact, the most beautiful church in the city. Having been in Johnstown longer than any ethnic group, excluding the Anglo-Saxon population, the Irish were a people on their way up the socio-economic ladder. A few of them had started to build their own businesses in the growing community. They also held most middle management positions in the factories of both Johnstown and Gloversville. There was an immediate conflict which arose between the Irish and the Sicilians, due to the issues that Sicilians brought to the labor market.

The north end of Johnstown was the Slovak part. The Slovaks formed a very large part of the Johnstown growth. They had their own church and, although not on the scale of the Irish church, was still a splendid edifice. These people came from Czechoslovakia, but they would not consider themselves part of that country. Once more, like the Sicilians, they would become a part of the large labor pool which would fuel the new glove companies and tanneries that grew into making these the largest and most prolific producers of leather gloves in the United States. Many second generation Slovaks would acquire great wealth in these very small communities. The western part of the town was known as the Flats and was inhabited mostly by recently immigrated Sicilians.

Chapter 16: Cayadutta and the Dark Cloud

It was September 9 when Guglielmo and Giuseppe stepped off the four corner trolley at the intersection of Main and Market Streets. From now on, they would be considered Americans and be referred to as William and Joe. They had to find Cayadutta Street, whose unusual name was derived from an Indian word. As they struggled with the difficult pronunciation of the street's name, Bill was wondering what sort of reception he would receive from his former fiancée, Rosalia and her husband, Sam, well known for his terrible and erratic outbursts of temper, and Bill feared serious antagonism when first they would meet. The English language was completely foreign to Joe, but Bill had mastered quite a lot of the language while he was in the army and did not have too many problems in obtaining clear directions as to where was West State Street Hill in the Flats.

Bill and Joe could not fail in noticing the three and four-story buildings that were along Main Street and the new roads under construction on Market and William Streets. Bill felt that this, as a small town, seemed like a quite prosperous place to begin a new life. The passers-by were smartly dressed and their gait was casual yet positive towards their intended destinations. One of the very significant things that Bill took note of was the fact that all these people were wearing shoes and he could only think of chances to ply his shoe-repairing trade and subsequently be able to earn enough money for his wife and daughters' passages to America. Having a certain wisdom garnered from his life's experiences, he knew that along the way he would have obstacles to overcome and people to struggle against in his attempt to rise above his present lowly status. Noticing that some bystanders were scrutinizing the two immigrants' clothes which were not like their own, Bill was undeterred knowing that his own strong mind and determined will would carry him through the upcoming times of good and bad. Trusting that the real test of a man begins in his mind, Bill would never, throughout his life in America, waver from this philosophy and his self-trust that he would always survive the storms that his new life would yield.

Walking down the State Street Hill, Bill and his companion, Joe, could not fail to notice the large ware-house like buildings which lined the north side of the street. These, they would later discover, were part of the Evans Glove Company which became like a second home for so many Sicilians who lived close by on the Flats. Observing the wonderful hard-working qualities of these strange immigrants, seemingly from another world, the two Evans cousins, Robert and Richard, had no qualms about hiring these new workers who would out-perform all others.

Paul Oliver, previously Oliveri, ran a fruit and vegetable stand on the corner of State and Cayadutta Streets. He was a big, robust man who ultimately, in Johnstown, became one of the wealthiest and most powerful of the Sicilian immigrants. Bill asked directions to Cayadutta Street and Mr. Oliveri pointed out the way to what would be the road to their future destinies.

A dark cloud of anticipation loomed over Bill as he climbed the steps to the front door of 16, Cayadutta Street. Rosalia, upon seeing the two, gave out a shout of joy and immediately embraced Bill. Her husband, Salvatore, was not at home at this moment, and working on his nocturnal business which seemed shady and which would later be revealed to the newcomers. His absence may have given Rosalia and Bill an opportunity to show each other the warmth of their feelings. After having been formally introduced to Bill's travelling partner, Joe, Rosalia offered them drinks and Italian cookies and was a gracious hostess.

When Sam finally came home, he did not show pleasure in seeing his brother-in-law, and was offended to see a stranger sitting in his living-room. When discussion of the two visitors staying at Sam and Rosalia's house arose, Sam proceeded to outline his rules and indicated that the house was already a bit crowded since they had their first child, Josephine and intended to have more children. Sam insisted that Joe could only stay for one night and that every day, Bill would have to be home by a certain time or he would find the door locked against him. Already, Bill was not feeling welcome and decided that his stay with the Salvatore's would be a short one.

Chapter 17: The Flats

Bill woke up late the next morning after his arrival. The sense of urgency which he was feeling was difficult to measure. Upon waking, he was happy to discover that Sam had left early for work and had taken Joe with him. Rosalia had made Bill a nice breakfast, and as he sat eating, he was struck by the house's large size and whose furniture was of a standard totally unimaginable back in the poverty-stricken Castelmola. He had seen beautiful objects in houses while he was a soldier, but he never thought that poor peasants could rise to the level of being able to afford such possessions for themselves. While conversing with Rosalia, it occurred to Bill that he should go to further explore the flats where so many immigrants were living and since this may be where he and his family, when they joined him, would no doubt end up. Upon finishing his breakfast, he thanked Rosalia, grabbed his Sicilian cap, and set off to explore the Flats.

At the present time, Sam was working in the Evans Tannery in Frogs Hollow, located at the end of West Montgomery Street and the factory had been constructed there because of its proximity to the Cayadutta Creek into which all of the tannery's wastes and dye stuffs poured out. The creek followed a course that led to the Mohawk River, causing it to become one of the most polluted rivers in the United States. This magnificent river, running the length of the Mohawk Valley, merged with the Hudson River and that too suffered the awful side-effects of pollution. For something like fifty years onwards, Gloversville and Johnstown factories continued be built close to the Cayadutta Creek and industrialists saved a fortune from not having to build waste-treatment plants.

The west side of town, the Flats, was located at the bottom of two hills, Main Street and State Street and the railroad ran parallel to Cayadutta Street. Cayadutta Street, whose name was Indian at the time of this saga, found itself populated with names such as: Oliveri, Alfano, Ruggeri, Rizzio, Melita, Greco, Cioffi, Cali, Brunetto, Valentino, Precopia, Cerrone, Garafola, Raneri, Lizio, Pappa, Fugazzatto and Fioravanti.

Just below where the railroad ran was the Cayadutta Creek and, as industry grew in Johnstown, and because the primary industries used color and dyes, manufacturers continued to find it free and convenient to dump all industrial waste into the Cayadutta Creek. As a youth, the author thought that it seemed natural to look out of a window and see the bright red or orange or even dark gray creek water meandering just below the garden. This pollution would eventually cause various problems for the inhabitants of the flats and present a challenge for them to solve. Agata Fioravanti herself solved this problem by employing sixteen cats, housed on her enclosed back porch, to patrol the property and keep it safe from rats which came up from the Cayadutta Creek. The house at 22, Cayadutta Street never saw rats within its confines.

It is important to mention one more name before Guglielmo and Giuseppe made their arrival in Johnstown. Richard and Robert Evans, two cousins, were the owners of a glove company that located on the State Street Hill and their company had an open door for many of the Sicilians who came to settle in the flats. As time passed, it became very well noted that the Evans family had been a God -Send for so many of the poor people who had come looking for a new and better life. As an aside, there was a story among Sicilians in the Flats that at one point, six or eight immigrants travelled to Albany to become naturalized citizens. When asked by the judge, "Who is the President of the United States?" In unison they all replied, "Richard Evans".

Starting his walk down Cayadutta Street, Bill passed a large Victorian house whose size, beautiful scroll work, and carving gave it a striking appearance. What a triumph it would be, he thought, if he could only become the owner of a house such as this! On his way he passed Burton Street and came to the corner where Paul Oliveri's fruit and vegetable stand stood. Bill proceeded to inquire as to whether or not Mr. Oliveri had knowledge of a store-front available for rent which would accommodate Bill's shoe repair business. Mr. Oliveri told him that on Washington Street, towards the end near to Perry Street, he would find a small store which he knew was suitable for Bill's needs.

Bill made his way to the store front and the Sicilian owner, who himself had only been in Johnstown for five years suggested that this rather-run down building might be what Bill wanted. The landlord, with his modest funds, had only been able to make superficial repairs to the building and was anxious to rent at a reasonable price. An agreement was made between the two, and Bill found himself ready to begin anew his shoe-repair business.

When Bill returned to the Salvatore house, he was informed that his travelling partner, Joe, with Sam's help, had landed a job at the Evans Tannery. He told Sam and

Rosalia what he had accomplished during the day. He believed that with his new found situation, he should be able to easily pay for his wife and young daughter's passages to America. Sam replied with a grunt, reminded Bill of his house rule, and then left to join some friends for a card game. Bill went to his room and began to compose a letter to Agata in Sicily:

Cara Agata:

Today I found a place to open my shoe-repair business. It will take some time, but soon I will be able to send you money to help you until I make enough to pay for your passage and for little Maria and Josephine to come to America.

When I finally have the money for you to come, I will also have a house and all the things we need to live inside that house. You must believe that anything is possible here and there is more than enough for all to share. Your sister has been very kind and generous to me and so far I've had no trouble with Sam. I don't know how long this will last but I only hope all will go well until I have enough money saved to rent a place of my own. Sam is a strange man and I never know what he is thinking. However, as you know, I believe that you can't escape your destiny and so when it ends here, it ends.

How are you, Maria and little Josephine getting along? I know you are strong and that you will not let anything or anyone harm you or our daughters. Please understand that I miss you all very much and only live for the day when you are all by my side in America. It will happen sooner than later. This I promise.

The time is late here and I must sleep for tomorrow I start my new business. Good night my love and Boca Lupo.

Love, Bill

After finishing the letter, Bill sealed the envelope, put it by his bedside, ready for posting the next day, and fell into a deep sleep.

Chapter 18: Changes

It had been six months since Bill had arrived in Johnstown and had opened his shoe-repair shop. He was beginning to realize that things had not turned out for him quite as he had expected. Income from the shop was meager and, after paying for his room and board and after sending just a few pennies to Agata in Castelmola, there was a pittance left over towards his dreams. He could barely save any extra money for his wife and daughter's passages and could hardly afford a pack of cigarettes. On this cold March morning of 1911, Bill had thoughts of having reached the end of the road. He felt hatred towards living with Sam and Rosalia and was discontent with his life as a cobbler. This poor state of affairs, however, was soon to change for him as good fortune may appear when least expected.

It was so bitterly cold when Bill reached the shop. He was absolutely freezing and, with a downed head and bended knees, he began the arduous task of lighting the old pot-bellied stove which sat in the center of the little room. For the next few hours, he was preoccupied with nursing the fire and for a short while began to lose sight of his sorrows. As the flames were steady and established and he could feel confident that the fire would not go out, the dark cloud of depression began to return. Just at this time a customer came through the door. It was Richard Evans, the joint owner of the Evans Tannery and the Evans Glove Factory who greeted Bill and handed over a pair of shoes which needed to be repaired. As Bill responded to Mr. Evans, the latter noticed Bill's rather uncommon proficiency in speaking English, and then he turned to leave. It was at that moment that he asked Bill about his satisfaction with a cobbler's life. Bill painted a somewhat dismal picture of his work and suggested that this would be the only kind of work he could do since he had no formal education. It was then that Mr. Evans offered him a job as a glove cutter. This would certainly change Bill's financial potential and his spirits rose when Mr. Evans said that, with Bill's experience and eye for detail, he had no doubt that he would be a great glove-cutter. Mr. Evans further boosted Bill's confidence by saying that his command of the English would make him a great asset in the factory when an interpreter was needed for the Italian and Sicilian workers. The new job offer was even more welcomed when Mr. Evans outlined the prospective wages. At this point, Bill could see so clearly that his wildest dreams for the future were going to come true and his belief in God, with His grand designs for life, was renewed.

Somewhat later in the day, the shop door opened again and in strode Joe Brunetto. With a downtrodden look on his face, he told Bill of his recent problems at work. Having left the Evans Tannery where the workers were picking on him, Joe had begun working at Karg's Tannery. This was the oldest tannery in New York State because of its proximity to the Adirondack Mountains where hunters killed deer, which lived there in plentiful numbers. Then the hunters needed to have the animal skins tanned. Deer skin was and still is, a very valuable commodity as it was and is still used, to the present time, in making coats and gloves. The animal meat even up to today, after a hundred years of hunting, remains a staple food in the area.

Bill was feeling a sense of elation about his new job offer and expressed his feelings to his friend who came to the shop asking Bill to visit the straw boss and speak on his behalf at Karg's Tannery, where problems were arising anew for him. Leaving the shoe-repair shop and locking the door, for what Bill believed to be his last time, the two set off for the tannery.

The tannery was close to Bill's shop, just down Perry Street, so the two arrived in a short time. Bill advised his friend to wait outside while he went inside. After having spoken to the office-manager, Bill was told to wait and he could overhear a conversation in which the office-manager told the boss, "There is a 'dago' in the hall waiting for you." When the boss came to talk he was quietly surprised at Bill's ability to speak English. The two went into the plant and Bill could immediately sense especially after hearing the slurs against immigrants that this encounter was not going to be a pleasant one. This boss was Irish and had lived in the community for many years and had perpetually retained his distaste for these "dagos" far too many of whom he felt were infiltrating the area.

In beginning the interview, Bill expressed that his friend, Joe, had trouble with the English language but felt sure that the boss had no reason to complain about Joe's hard-working traits and that he just had problems following instructions because of the language barrier. This inability to understand what was being said to him, made the boss feel quite justified in tormenting Joe. Little did the boss know that Joe, seemingly vulnerable, had power and pride and could easily break this man like a dry twig. When Bill explained the reason for his visit, quite unexpectedly and quite alarmingly, he grabbed Bill, slapped his face, knocked him against the wall and told him never again to show his face at the tannery. This was such an extremely harrowing, humiliating and embarrassing experience for Bill that when his Sicilian cap flew off his head in the attack and fell in a puddle near to the loading dock, he refused to pick it up, left it on the ground, and from that day on, he never wore a Sicilian cap again.

Joe asked Bill what the outcome of the meeting had been and, not wanting his friend to feel more distressed, was vague in his answers. He simply suggested that he should be patient for very shortly a new more satisfying and far less aggravating job would be coming to him. Bill was sure of this.

Joe suggested that the two go for a drink to celebrate the good things that had happened that day. They decided upon the Waterway Bar which was so-named because of its proximity to the water of the Cayadutta Creek. After a few drinks, they lost track of time and it was way past ten o'clock when they began their walk home. When Bill tried Sam and

Rosalia's door, he found it locked against him and there was no doubt at all in his mind that his relationship with them must come to a close. Not being able to suffer the bitter cold outside, he found safe haven with Paul Oliveri for the night and thereupon made a vow to himself that he would somehow try to obtain a place of his own and never more be at the mercy of others.

During the past week, Bill had noticed a "For Rent" sign on the door of a house at 22, Cayadutta Street. Having learned that the house was owned by a Jonah Hess, he set out to find this man with whom he struck a deal which allowed Bill to move in right away. Walking through the front door and over the threshold was an exhilarating experience. Bill knew, really knew at last, that this was where his fresh, exciting, fulfilling life as a Sicilian immigrant was truly going to begin.

Chapter 19: The Banner Year

Feeling completely overwhelmed at what seemed to Bill like a reversal in his fortune he could see the favorable move of having gone out of 16, Cayadutta Street, and into number 22. In most cases, one is in and then one is out, but in Bill's case it was just the opposite. He found himself out of the shoe repair business and into the Evans Glove Company, and money was out of his pocket and into the bank. He thought that his life could not get any better, but later he would see that it did.

One day, a different Sicilian man, newly dressed in a bowler hat and a handsome top coat, appeared at 22 Cayadutta Street. The new man had shed his Sicilian garb and acquired a new suit, a bowler hat, and a handsome top coat. Bill had bought several white shirts and dress pants for his new position at the glove factory, where in those early days, all glove-cutters were required to wear white shirts and decent trousers, and they took great pride in their work and in their appearance. This may be something not to be so readily seen among today's labor force.

Bill rapidly learned the glove-cutting trade as he was a natural at the work and he made Mr. Evans's predictions come true. At this time, gloves were pre-cut in factories and then sent to women glove sewers who did the work in their own homes. So many of the sewers readily looked forward to and appreciated the gloves which had been cut by Bill Fioravanti since he was so careful and detailed in his work, and this made the women's sewing so much easier. By the end of the decade, the practice of glove assembly in homes would cease to exist and all the sewing would be done in factories.

Although Bill enjoyed his work very much, his biggest satisfaction was the house where he was now residing at 22, Cayadutta Street. Although he was a renter, this was the first dwelling that even resembled a complete house. At the time when he had moved in, the house was divided and there were tenants living up, and he was living down, but the house was so big that he had six rooms which was a dream come true for a poor man from such a faraway place.

So many happenings would eventually take place in that house for the Fioravanti family which are worthy of description. The house was built in Victorian times with a total of seventeen rooms as well as a large cellar and an enormous attic. The oak woodwork was plentiful and many of the walls had wanes-coating on them and unusual for the time, there were bathrooms both up and down. However, the house itself was in a most shabby condition and Bill made a vow to himself that, at a later date when he was the owner, he would set about fixing it up and make it a showplace on the street. At this time, the property boasted a large barn in its back yard which was very close to the creek. The present owner, Jonah Hess, having enough financial strains himself, was certainly not going to take care of the house's needs and wanted to relieve himself of it. Bill would have to wait to do the repairs himself when hopefully, if his plan worked out, the property belonged to him.

It was during the decade from 1910 to 1920 that all the major members of the Fioravanti family would be in place and along with other Sicilians, Irish, Slovak and Anglo-Saxons would all be entrenched for many years to come in what would be the heart and soul of Johnstown, New York.

Bill Fioravanti saw himself surging upwards in to the future of America. He was to be one of those trying to make it the true melting pot of the world. Nevertheless, at this point, before he fulfilled all his future goals, his greatest achievement was in leaving the residence of Sam Valentino and saving money to bring over his little family. Later he would think of bringing over his dear brother, whom he felt, himself, deserved an opportunity to share in Bill's dreams and good fortune. Once all these goals had been nothing but empty dreams, but now, Halleluiah!

Chapter 20: Family

Two years passed by and, even though Bill's life had taken a turn for the better he had endured his share of extreme loneliness and severe depression. Life was still a struggle yet Bill was feeling optimistic that he had been able to save enough money for Agata and their daughters' passages to America. The tickets for the family were now paid for and his wife and children, Maria and Josephine, arrived in New York on August 12, 1912. Bill was waiting at the dock for them and, after much kissing and embracing, the four made their way to the station where they boarded a train for Fonda.

After leaving Sicily, Agata was to be exposed to a life totally beyond her imagination. All her life she had lived in a crowded one-room house with her parents and three sisters. What a feeling of exaltation she would have when she gazed upon her new residence at 22 Cayadutta Street; a palace compared to where she had lived before! One may never know such feelings as Agata experienced since it is difficult to grasp the totality of poverty which she had just left behind in the old country.

As the train moved onwards, Bill was deep in his thoughts of what he had achieved up to this point and yet was contemplating how he could amass enough funds to bring his brother to America. He believed that the present arrival of his wife would certainly help if she were prepared to learn how to sew gloves which she ultimately did and proved herself most capable of taking care of children, tending to a large house and being a productive glove sewer.

For some unknown reason, Sicilian women when they came to America, maintained their original names and did not Anglicize them as did the men. Agata would be referred to by her family and friends as Donida, a combination of "Donna" and "Ida", and one of the author's sisters would later take her name of Agatha.

In her new country, Donida gave birth to two sons. The first of these was William Fioravanti 11, born on May 2, 1913, and the second was Constantino, who took the nick-name of Louie. This family was to remain intact until the forties and would try to survive in a country where they too believed all was possible. There was a particular problem that Bill Fioravanti 1 overlooked in his zest for America. This concerned how much anxiety his children, born of immigrant parents, would have to endure. The community, as a whole, embraced new immigrants in the workplace but they were rarely socially accepted. Their children, while attending school, also suffered terrible insults and punishments from teachers who were from German, Irish and English stock and considered the students to be inferior to them, and undesirables. On one particular occasion, a Fioravanti boy was viciously chastised by the elementary school principal from the school in the Flats. A close friend of the family, who had no qualms about making a complaint on the child's behalf, went to the principal to register to complain. This lady did not look half-Italian and half Polish as was her heritage, and the principal mistakenly thought that she was German or some person of importance. Mrs. Teal, the principal, began to insult the immigrant children, referring to them as "no good" and "just like their parents," thereupon the family friend threatened Mrs. Teal that, should she ever again treat the Fioravanti member in such a disparaging way, she, the principal, would find herself flying through the window which, by the way, happened to be on the` second-floor. Bill Fioravanti had absolutely no awareness of the teachers' attitudes and continued to believe in his new-found American paradise where he was free to be almost whatever or whomever he wanted. However, his personal expectations did not correlate with those which he had for his children, and he never truly grasped the torment which they, especially his sons, were forced to endure. It was 1913 and very significant for Bill as he had succeeded in saving enough money for his brother's passage. It was also a very auspicious year for New York itself which was holding the celebrated Armory Show from February 17 to March 15. The exhibition was the first one of its kind to show so many works of art together in one place from Europe and from the United States. Painters such as Renoir, Monet, Picasso and Van Gogh were on display and introduced New Yorkers, previously accustomed to realism, to the new art of modernism. It was this extraordinary event that caused Bill to delay booking his brother's passage and subsequently, Giuseppe Andreana, the brother from afar, did not arrive in New York until September 11 of that year.

When Giuseppe arrived, he brought with him his wife, Josephine and their son Vincent. He found that his brother, in anticipation and because of his increasing funds, had managed to rent both floors in the house at 22, Cayadutta Street and having so many beloved family members around him, would prevent him from ever again feeling dreadful bouts of loneliness and depression.

Life to Bill and his family continued to show great promise. It was a time of prosperity in Johnstown. The glove businesses were flourishing and Knox Gelatin, a manufacturer of granulated unflavored gelatin, employed close to a hundred people. The Knox family, owners of this large factory, would become wonderful benefactors to the Johnstown community and the decade certainly seemed to be a never-ending river of advancement. This would all change as the decade reached its final years.

PART TWO

Chapter 21: Touched

During the early years after the arrival of his brother and his family, Bill Fioravanti thought he had built a strong foundation for his future. Bill now had two sons born to Agata in America, and his brother's wife gave him a son named Joseph Andreana 11, born in January of 1914. Young Joe would have a horrendous childhood but would grow up to be one of the most decent men imaginable. Little did Bill know that his brother's wife, unlike Agata, found the strange new land extremely hard to bear with its harsh winters and she certainly would have returned to Sicily had it not been for her husband whom she dearly loved. The winters in the early part of the century were particularly severe with snow storms so intense that roads were almost invisible over the tall snow-banks, but the warm season of spring and the pleasant cool, sunny fall weather would somehow compensate for the severity of winter.

Johnstown, with its streets, lined with majestically tall maple and pine trees that seemed to climb up to the sky, was magnificent at this time. Bill was in love with the town, and Donida never even entertained a single thought of returning to Sicily. She felt like a duchess in her large house and carefully guarded it as if her life depended on it and never forgot the awful poverty which she had endured back in her native land.

By now, Bill had become so proficient in the English language that he could easily write and speak it fluently. He had a comprehensive knowledge of the English grammar which would make it hard for him to be tricked by others who were trying to take advantage, and he had this in mind when he was soon to be considering making an offer to Jonah Hess with regards to buying the house on 22, Cayadutta Street.

War has a way of touching everybody in one way or another. Although he was living on the other side of the world, the Italian Government called up Joseph Andreana to be drafted into the army. Not acquiescing to this call would make Joseph a traitor and bring him the risk of trial and imprisonment. Bill, on the other hand, was never called to serve and this may have been due to the fact that he had already previously served in the Italian Army.

World War 1 had begun in the summer of 1914 and in 1915. Italy had joined in the fight. Late that year, Joseph left for Italy, and his brother Bill was extremely distraught since he had a premonition that the two would never meet again. After Joseph left, his wife, who was pregnant at the time, returned to Sicily and it is uncertain as to whether or not she ever saw her husband again before he was killed at the tender age of thirty-nine. When Bill's sister-in-law returned to Sicily, she found it impossible to cope with raising three children and placed her two sons in an orphanage. Very scant information of the Andreana family was learned until, seventeen years later. Bill Fioravanti made arrangements to bring young Joseph Andreana back to America before his citizenship would be eliminated when he turned eighteen years of age. The other two Andreana children remained behind in Sicily. Having dealt with his brother's departure and that of his sister-in-law and her children, Bill now turned his energy towards the purchase of 22, Cayadutta Street. What subsequently ensued is akin to a biblical drama!

Chapter 22: The Baptist

The nineteenth century had been more than generous to the British since they had acquired most of what became to be known as the British Empire. With their increase in territorial horizons, the British were reinventing and perfecting the art of diplomacy and it has long been noted that what happens first sociologically in England, eventually surfaces here in America. Although it has been very difficult for the United States to duplicate the British diplomatic skills, a close watch has always been kept. As the century was drawing to a close and England was beginning to lose hold of parts of its empire, it carefully learned to adapt to the many changes which were occurring. This accommodation, as it should be called, was what Americans saw and grasped and, although it took a longer time in America, it was copied and became a way of life for the so-called upper middle-class and aristocracy of this country.

Bill Fioravanti did not belong to either the American middle-class or to the American aristocracy, but even as a simple immigrant, he quickly learned the rules of accommodation. He had been wrestling backwards and forwards with Jonah Hess in an attempt to purchase the house at 22, Cayadutta Street and they seemed to come to an impasse because of Bill's being a Catholic. Jonah was himself a Baptist and, although desperate for money, was totally unwilling to sell to one of a different faith as him. After much wrangling, Jonah made Bill Fioravanti an outrageous offer. He would agree to the price which Bill was willing to pay for the house on the condition that the latter would convert to the Baptist faith. Some time elapsed and, on one cold February afternoon and in an attempt to make the sale, Jonah Hess waited for Bill outside the Evans Glove Company. Bill had been carefully considering Jonah's previous offer and, as the two men walked together towards Cayadutta Street, said that he had decided to the conditions of sale. Jonah was extremely shocked that his offer was being accepted since he was aware of the strong ties which most Sicilians and Italians had to the Catholic Church and thought he might have to seek another buyer for the house. He, as a Baptist himself, had total allegiance to his own religion and would understand another rejection by Bill. It was however, surprisingly agreed at that time that Bill was willing to agree to pay a certain sum of money to Jonah who would then go ahead and arrange for the baptism. The only real problem that Bill now had was in trying to come up with the money.

The Oliveri's, or Oliver's as they were now called, had a cousin who lived on School Street, half-way up the West Main Street Hill, just above the Flats. The cousin was Boom-Boo-Brunetto who had become quite prosperous through buying and selling houses and by owning and operating a successful social club where immigrants came to drink and gamble. Paul Oliver advised Bill to request a loan from him.

Boom-Boo knew Bill quite well and trusted his word and appeared receptive when asked for the loan. It was with just a handshake that the $2,300 was given to Bill who was now almost ready to close on the house. The baptism was arranged for the Sunday before the house closing which was set for February 23, 1917. For the baptism at the church at the top of West State Street, since he would be submerged under water, Bill was to wear clean underwear in preparation for the ceremony.

That memorable Sunday of the baptism was bitterly cold. Bill feared that God was sending such awful weather since He was angry at bill's decision.   Upon reaching the Baptist church, Jonah took his aspiring convert inside who then stripped down to his underwear and was given a white robe to wear.   Bill was then directed to the great brass, ornately-decorated - font and directed to stand inside it. The ceremony took place and Bill affirmed his belief and trust in Jesus Christ and was submerged in the holy water in the, "Name of the Father and of the Son, and of the Holy Spirit." The ceremony was short and after a few congratulations, Bill left and was on his way down the hill to what was his now own home of which he was the sole owner.

Going down the hill, Bill felt like Sisyphus only he was feeling happy and not in perpetual agony. He thought of all the improvements that he intended for the house to restore its beauty and planned to get in touch with the reputed best carpenter in Johnstown whose name was Mr. Cali, who also lived on Cayadutta Street. He knew that Mr. Cali, in making the house into a one-family dwelling, would do such splendid work that it would make Bill's new property the best looking house on the street.

Chapter 23: The Transformation and the Master-Builder

It is not unreasonable to give George Cali, the Master Builder, most of the credit for transforming the Flats. His contribution was seen in many houses that were being restored on Cayadutta Street and in other surrounding areas. George was a simple man with a rare gift for building. He was an immigrant from the small Sicilian town of Graniti, and he had married a widow with several children and they all resided at 29, Cayadutta Street. Bill Fioravanti was one of the first to hire George Cali and he first began renovating the house's interior. It was not long before the beautiful oak woodwork and the wooden wanes coating began to shine and spring to life, and the house was totally converted into a one family residence rather than two. The outside of the house was given a fresh coat of white paint and a vineyard that bore purple grapes in the summer was built in the back garden. Bill made his own wine from the harvest and was the only immigrant in the neighborhood to have the luxury of their own vineyard. Nearly all of the houses on Cayadutta Street were having facelifts but none as elegant as Bill Fioravanti's house. The Greco's and the Rizzio's were all neighbors who were trying to upgrade their houses.

Along with renovating the dwellings, most of the Sicilians took great pride in planting long rectangular gardens at the back of the houses which stretched right down to the Cayadutta Creek. The rectangular vegetable gardens were like works of art and the immigrants worked them like master painters. They were a sight to behold and so beautiful compared to the contour land which they had farmed back in the old country.

Years were flying by and in 1919, the Volstead Act, the 18th amendment was a federal law and drinking was outlawed in every state in the Union. To most Italians and Sicilians this did not pose much of a problem as they were not big drinkers and made their own wine, but to others it was a chance to make money with illegal stills and many would become very rich. One group of people who profited greatly from illegal distilling was the Benjamin Melita family who were bootleggers with prosperous customers from many surrounding towns such as Canajoharie and Little Falls which were big manufacturing areas where people could easily afford to pay for alcohol and spend time in the speakeasies.

By 1920 many of the glove companies were installing sewing machines in their factories. The American workforce was now radically changed as women ceased sewing in their own homes and went to work in the factories.

On April 24, 1921, a certain Mr. Piccione arrived from Avella, a small Sicilian town near to Siracusa, bringing with him a five year old girl named Carmella Caraco and her two year infant brother, Gaetano Caraco. Carmella, known as Millie, would eventually marry Arthur Aulisi who was to become a lawyer and judge. Arthur's son, Richard, would follow in his father's footsteps and rise to the position of Supreme Court Judge. Mr. Piccione would also summon a friend from Avella who was later to have a big impact on the Fioravanti family.

Chapter 24: The Stranger

The arrival in Johnstown of Mr. Piccione and his two wards was a quiet low-key appearance. They, unlike most Sicilians, did not go straight to the Flats which by this time was getting over crowded, but went to family members who were waiting for them on Clinton Street where many Sicilians had now chosen to live Later, some of the second generation would hang out together and play harmless sports like football and baseball and form a gang called "The Clinton Street Pirates". Although by this time, Clinton Street was becoming more populated, the western part of Johnstown, which included streets such as Burton, Wells, and Melcher, was still dominated primarily with Sicilians whose names included the Precopio's, the Costa's, the Samperi's and the Marchetti's.

As soon as Mr. Piccione was settled, he wrote a letter to his old Sicilian friend, Michael Mazzaro, who was living in New York City and working as a shoe designer for a big company. According to Ellis Island documents, Michael Mazzaro had arrived in New York in October, 1912 which meant that he had been residing for about seven years in the big city. In retrospect, this appears out of character for him since he would later show a very strong attachment to the small town of Johnstown and could never seem to leave it for any extended period of time. The Ellis Island Manifesto indicated that Michael was married, but there never was any visible proof of this, and he certainly did not mention any wife when he came to live with the Fioravanti's.

Mr. Piccione became a glove cutter and through this trade came to know Bill Fioravanti. At this time, Michael Mazzaro was living with Mr. Piccione who saw there might be a strong intellectual connection and compatibility between Bill and Mike. Both men were very literate. They enjoyed books and opera, and were men of integrity, and Bill Fioravanti had so much extra space in his large house that there would be plenty of room for a new tenant. Extra income from a boarder would also alleviate Bill's expenses, as the glove business had begun to slow down due to a post-war recession which was beginning to grow. Although times were tougher than they previously were, the Fioravanti's and many others, including factory owners and banks, all managed to overcome difficulties by which they were slowly being confronted.

As the door-bell rang at 22, Cayadutta Street, Donida answered and found herself face to face with a well-dressed tall, slender man whose complexion was strangely pallid. At first she was a little taken aback but, on looking into Mike's eyes, she felt he had an ethereal way about him as if he were from another world and as if he could see deep into her soul.

Bill came to the door to greet Mike and proceeded to welcome him inside and show him the bedroom which would be his. After meeting the children, who had been peering around the corner of the kitchen in an attempt to get a good view of the visitor, and after some refreshment and conversation, it was established quite clearly that Bill and Mike were surely kindred spirits and that Donida, the children and the two men, would together form an everlasting bond. There was no sense whatsoever, reflected by any family member, that the new tenant would in any way be considered an intruder. His acceptance was immediate and he would remain, until his death many years later, an important part of the Fioravanti family unit.

The new tenant loved to write poetry, had lasting patience to explain things to the children who came to love him dearly, and had lively discussions with Bill. Together, they seemed just like brothers who had earned the love and respect of the entire Fioravanti family.

The early years of the decade saw a general reduction in prosperity. Soldiers had marched on Washington to demand pensions, trade was difficult since banks were not readily lending money, and in Johnstown and Gloversville the shortage of deer had an impact on the glove industry. The Evans Glove Company stayed alive but was struggling, and most immigrants somehow made it through. All of a sudden, the pendulum seemed to swing in the other direction and companies such as Gates and Mills, Superb, Boyce and Lazarus and Fownes, the old English company, started to improve. Many tanneries, such as Blyels, Peerless, Wood and Hyde, and small ones like the Cleary Tannery began to show signs of an upward swing. Along with all these developments was the introduction of the sewing machine into the factories. Most families were being affected as the women and young daughters went out of the house and into the factory.

The Fioravanti family was flourishing again and the addition of Mike Mazzaro, whom it was later discovered was from an aristocratic family in Avella, brought so much joy to them and especially to his dear friend, Bill, who thought of him as a didactic being and such a great teacher and loyal companion. The Stranger, who had come to join his soul-mates, was a stranger no more.

Chapter 25: The Ruggeri's

The Ruggeri's are an important part of this story as one of them, Mary Ruggeri, born in 1916, was the author's mother. Tom and Nunziata Ruggeri's first children were sons. The oldest was Frank, nick-named "Blackie", and then Tony. The family first settled in a house on School Street which was one of the many houses on the street owned by Boom Boo Brunetto. Tom's brother, Dominic, lived on that street for decades.

Once they arrived in America, the family first settled in another New York State town near to Albany, called Bethlehem, where Tom worked as a stone-crusher, using shear brute force to survive. The Ruggeri's would later relocate to Johnstown where the family added two more daughters, Mary, the author's mother, Josephine, and two more sons, Philip and Joseph, also known as "Ace."

Having little or no skills, Tom was forced to work as a laborer in the wet part of a tannery and this was considered by all to be one of the dirtiest, thankless jobs imaginable, but Tom had no choice with so many mouths to feed. Every time he came home from the tannery he was covered from head to toe in colored dyes and chemicals which today are considered highly toxic. Tom had no choice and only survived through his incredible strength. He even lived up to his eighties, which is quite remarkable considering the punishment which was meted out to him for so many years at work.

In time, the Ruggeri's were sadly evicted from the house on School Street and found shelter at 14 Cayadutta Street, just four houses from the Fioravanti's and this would cause a dramatic change in Mary's life. Donida was suspicious of those outside her family but fell in love with Mary, who was treated like family and who would spend most of her time with the Fioravanti's. She continued to be like a permanent figure in the household and this would later lead to more serious consequences as she was feeling herself a more successful immigrant than poor Nunziata. Donida seemed to take her under her wing along with the daughter, Mary, and became her protector.

The house where the Ruggeri's had moved to on Cayadutta Street was owned by a family called Buckingham who passionately hated Sicilians and Italians. They were owners of land on Cayadutta Street which stretched from Warren to Main Street, and on the corner of Main and Cayadutta Streets, they were the proprietors of a convenience store where Mrs. Buckingham sold foods and other sundries. Being a most ungracious woman, on one occasion when Tom Ruggeri could not pay the rent and his belongings were strewn out onto the street, Donida Fioravanti decided to approach Mrs. Buckingham to plead a case for the Ruggeri's who now had no place to live. Forgetting her inability to speak English, Donida spoke her words in Italian, and Mrs. Buckingham was so fiercely outraged that she proceeded to pull a gun out from under the counter and pointed it in Donida's direction, threatening to shoot. Recognizing the heat of the situation, Donida promptly retreated and waited for her husband, Bill, to come home from the glove factory. Being the kind and caring person that he was, Bill helped the family to find a place to live on Burton Street and gave them money to help them get a fresh start. He could never forget the pitiful poverty which he had known himself back in Sicily and was not going to let another Sicilian starve to death if he could help it. This would be one of so many charitable deeds that Bill Fioravanti would do in his lifetime. He was indeed a special person.

Chapter 26: Life Is Good

By 1928, Bill Fioravanti had settled into what would become the rest of his life. He now had a big family together with a beautiful home and his friend, Michael Mazzaro, provided him with all the intellectual stimulation he needed to maintain an active mind. His sons, Bill and Louie, were teenagers and going through the usual rites that young people experience during growth. His two daughters, Mary and Josephine, were working in the Boyce and Lazarus Glove Company. The girls were bringing home money and Michael Mazzaro was not only paying rent and helping with the finances but he was like a surrogate father to all four children. His wife, Donida, had help in the house with little Mary Ruggeri who was constantly with the family. Bill Fioravanti had changed jobs and now worked in Gloversville for the Rubin Glove Company. All in all, life could not get much better for Bill and his family.

It was at about this time that, with the respect which he had earned from the community, people began to refer to him as Don Guglielmo and Michael Mazzaro was now called Don Michael. They were thought of as very special men.

While the girls were working hard and contributing to the family, the two sons were seemingly not expected to do the same. Louie and his friend, Joe Brunetto, a son of one of the older Bill Fioravanti friends, spent most of their time robbing local stores and chasing girls. Louie and Joe focused their attention on stealing from Sponnable's Grocery store and from Oliver's Fruit Company while young Bill had other things on his mind. He had developed a strong love for automobiles and, even though under the age for driving, with the help of his companion, Frank Ruggeri, who bore no relation to young Mary Ruggeri's family, would frequently roll the older Bill Fioravanti's enticing Pierce Arrow out of the driveway and be off for a ride. They were never deterred from stealing the car since little punishment was meted out to them after their youthful escapades.

Economically, the country was not doing well, but most of the Sicilians in Johnstown and the Neapolitans in Gloversville always seemed to find a way to survive. It would be safe to say that the immigrants were extremely resourceful.

With the advent of sewing machines in the factories, the mainstream work force had changed dramatically since women now went inside the factories to sew. Because of their ethnic heritage, the women were put in precarious positions, being harassed with obscenities, ethnic slurs and sexual intimidation. A Mr. Joyce, brother to the then Chief of Police, was a prime offender of this kind of harassment, and he felt very secure with his brother's position and thought himself immune from any punishment. In reality, his assessment was in some way correct, since his brother was feared by the community, but he failed to take into account other forthcoming reprisals for his actions and continued to push women to the very limit.

One dark night in autumn, Joyce was walking home from work and about to cross the railroad tracks on Main Street, just below Meadow Street. Suddenly, two men appeared out of the darkness, jumped on him, and cut his throat from ear to ear. Lucky for him, he survived this attempted murder, but was quick to learn that it was foolish to harass Sicilian girls and ceased his intimidating behavior. The chief of Police, his brother, irate and infuriated, tried to track down the perpetrators, but got no help from the community who felt his brother had received what he deserved. After this incident, rumors flew that the two attackers had been hired in Utica, New York, by the Falcone brothers who were just beginning their ascent as the Upstate Mafia. They would eventually rule over the Upstate mobs far into the fifties and would be discovered at the famous "Appalachian Mafia Convention".

Rising and smoldering out of the weak economic situation in Gloversville and Johnstown, was another group which was about to become notorious in the coming years. The two central figures of this group, Tom Lizio and Sam Valentino, were about to create an organization that would reach citizens of both good and bad repute and, together, they would literally light up the sky.

With all going on around him, Don Guglielmo Fioravanti and his good friend, Don Michael, would carry on as if all aspects of life were wonderful. Delving into their hearts and souls, only a picture of pure and enlightened beings would emerge. Their good life was soon to be in contrast to the fiery times ahead.

Chapter 27: The Good Samaritan

It came to pass that a man of slight stature, named Tom Lizio, bought the property on West State Street, two lots down from the Evans Glove Company buildings. He was a good man who thrived and prospered in his new surroundings.   Tom had started out as a barber and his success from this enabled him to open a store that dealt in dry goods, vegetables, and Italian delicacies. He seemed to rise up at such a rate that, at times, it looked as if a higher power was assisting him in his good fortune. As it turned out, he was being assisted, but this had nothing to do with a superior power. Tom's success was being helped by an associate who would eventually lead Tom down a path of confusion and turmoil.

The land which Tom had acquired was a very large piece of property which stretched from West State Street to where the Cayadutta Creek curved around and finally touched Cayadutta Street before flowing into the   Mohawk River. On this land were two enormous dwellings. The front building, standing on West State Street, was a two story structure which housed the barber shop and the grocery store. Tom and his family lived above and, with a wife and their six children, ample room remained for them all to live in comfort.   At the back of the house was a dwelling that can be best described as an enormous wooden warehouse which had living quarters, presently unoccupied, that stretched across the entire top floor. Initially, Tom had little use for the whole space, but, eventually, there would be a day, however, through the success of his later part-time business, that he would find more and more use for it, and later on, one of Tom's sons would live there and raise his family over the warehouse.

Tom Lizio had a large family to support and he did it in a very elegant way. His wife, Josephine and their six children lacked for nothing and, for the times, Tom himself seemed like an old feudal Baron from the old country. However, there was a big difference between Tom and the Barons. He was not an exploiter of his people but was a man of such good character that he was beloved by all Sicilians who frequented his establishment. The author's grandfather, Tom Ruggeri, who so many times could not feed his family, was just one of the poor souls that Tom Lizio reached out to help by advancing credit and giving food without ever haunting for payment. The author's mother, Mary Ruggeri, frequently relayed this generosity to the author that they would have starved had it not been for the Samaritan, Tom Lizio. So many poor Sicilian immigrants, finding it hard to survive in the Fulton County recession, benefitted from this great magnanimous spirit.

Tom's oldest child, Sam, would ultimately become one of Bill Fioravanti 11's closest friends and would eventually play a big part in the lives of all members of the Fioravanti family. It is a sad thing to say, however, that the wonderful reputation of he who had given so much hope and support to so many suffering people, would later be soiled by notoriety and come to have a double meaning when it came to the name of Tom Lizio, Good Samaritan.

Chapter 28: 1931: The Fanatical Year

Bill Fioravanti had just sat down at the head of the table in the large dining room of 22, Cayadutta Street. Mike Mazzaro was pouring white wine which he and Bill had made a few months ago in the cellar of the house. It was the first day of January, 1931, and the whole family was seated around the large oval oak table. All family members were preparing to celebrate the New Year with a bountiful meal and with a toast given by Don Michael and Don Guglielmo. Donida was scurrying back and forth from the kitchen and bringing back many foods which had been specially prepared for this auspicious occasion. The entire scene was a joy to behold. However, there had already been many changes in the lives of the family players, and not all of these had made Don Guglielmo proud or content.

Young Bill, now eighteen years of age, had quit school two years previously and was learning to cut gloves with his father at the Rubin Glove Company. This was a great disappointment to his father who had hoped that he would go off to college. His younger son, Louie, had also left school early and was working as a floor-walker at the Boyce and Lazarus Company. His daughters, Maria and Josephine, had left the same company and were now employed at the Denkert Sport Glove Shop making footballs, basketballs, baseball gloves, and boxing gloves. The new work was much harder than making dress gloves as they had done at their previous job, but the close proximity of the workplace to 22, Cayadutta Street was very desirable and this was what later enticed Mary and Josephine Fioravanti and later Mary Ruggeri, the author's mother to work at the same company. All three women would eventually work in that company for most of their lives.

As the New Year's Day meal progressed, Bill could not help looking through the bay windows at the far end of the dining room and seeing the old barn that he thought to be an enormous eye-sore, staring back at him in the face. This same barn had brought some income to the family as a certain Buck Ramsey, a junk-garbage-collector, used to board his horses inside the barn and paid money for this service. This same man would eventually own the Johnstown Hotel on Main Street, which was to become one of the most prominent buildings in the town, and he himself was a man way ahead of the times since, years later, men would kill each other over the option to collect garbage. As he continued to view the barn, which was visible through the window, Bill Fioravanti made a decision that the author believed to be the only illegal one which his grandfather ever made.

The family meal ended on a pleasant note with Italian pastries and good wishes for a bright and prosperous New Year. Little did Bill and Mike Mazzaro know that this particular New Year would be fraught with problems of pain, sufferings of conscience, and some small feeling of success!

By 1931, America was two years into what would come to be called "The Great Depression", and was one year away from the enactment and Twenty First Amendment, known as "The Blaine Act" which repealed "The Volstead Act" which had initialized prohibition. It was rumored that in the following year young Bill Fioravanti and his friend, Sam Lizio, would be the first to bring in a truck-load of legitimate beer to Fulton County It has been difficult to substantiate this story, but it did serve to enhance young Bill's reputation in so far as he would eventually be respected for his ability to solve problems and for his courage to take risks in the workingman's world.

"The Great Depression" never seemed, in general, to have a large effect on the people of Fulton County. Some manufacturers, however, such as the Evans Glove Company, were showing signs of failure and did eventually fail, but with foresight and business acumen, the Richard Evan's family reinvented themselves and developed a flourishing textile business, one of America's oldest industries. They would rise to new heights once more and this time would maintain their high status for decades to come. This was the background to "The Fanatical Year" into which Bill Fioravanti was entering.

Josephine Andreana, Bill Fioravanti's sister-in-law, finding the harsh upstate winters too hard to bear, followed her husband, who had been drafted into the Italian army, and left America to return to Sicily. Being pregnant at the time, upon arriving in Palermo in 1916, Josephine gave birth to a daughter whom she named Mary. Seemingly all of a sudden, this poor woman found herself burdened with three children, two boys and a girl, and no way to locate her husband for any kind of financial help. She could barely support herself, let alone three young children.

As war was looming and fascists were visible in all parts of Italian and Sicilian society, poor Josephine, with little or no income, was dependant mostly upon the help from her own family and friends who lived in Palermo on the opposite end of Sicily to Castelmola where her husband had been born. She made what she felt to be an unavoidable decision which would affect both of her two sons, Vincent and Joseph. They would be placed in an orphanage in Palermo.

For about sixteen years, these two boys lived in a very undesirable and harsh orphanage. When Vincent became eighteen, he was released to join the Italian Army and his brother, Joseph, would remain impounded in the orphanage for at least two more years. Nevertheless, somehow word came to Joseph that, since he had been born in America, and was thus an American citizen, if he could return to his birthplace before his eighteenth birthday, he could maintain his American citizenship and live in America. It was January 25th, and Joe turned seventeen years of age. Somehow through securing his Uncle Bill's address in Johnstown, America, he wrote requesting help to pay for his passage to America and for his sponsorship upon arrival. His uncle agreed to help, secured passage for his nephew on the Conte Biancomano which was to depart from the Port of Naples in late April, 1931 and would arrive in New York on May 4, of the same year.

The curious events that led up to Joe's departure and how he came to initiate and solve all the complex problems that a young boy of seventeen had to overcome are what are the real enigma of Joe's adventure. It is possible that the son and daughter, whom he would later have, were more knowledgeable about their father's journey than the author is privy to. Joe, like his father and uncle did possess an intelligence which had been handed down to Giuseppe and Guglielmo. The irony of it all was that the children lived in a world where circumstance and history short changed them, and it would take another book to try to explain just what those circumstances were. Notwithstanding, Giuseppe Andrea Andreana was met by his uncle, Bill Fioravanti, in New York in May and thus was to begin a new life in America.

On a cold March day, prior to greeting his nephew, Bill Fioravanti Sr. decided that he would stop at Tom Lizio's for a hair-cut. While Bill was getting the hair-cut, he happened to mention to Tom what an ugly eye-sore the old barn was at the end of his property, and he also casually slipped into the conversation the amount of insurance which he was carrying which included the barn, Tom finished the haircut and understood what was being suggested.. Bill left the barber's shop and knew that, for the first time in his life, he was about to engage in an illegal act. This would be the one and only time when Bill Fioravanti would knowingly break the law and his conscience was plagued by this for the rest of his life. He constantly worried that his name might be connected to the events which would later transpire.

On a very rainy night at the beginning of April, the Fioravanti family was awakened by a bright light in the back yard. This turned out to be the blaze which would level the old barn. By morning, the barn itself was just rubble spread out over the yard. With the barn gone, Bill collected on the insurance. Little information transpired as to how much insurance money was gathered from this fire, but within two weeks, the Master Builder, Mr. George Cali, was laying out plans for a new garage, which was to hold four cars and have the latest accordion doors. In a very short period of time, the new garage was built like a fortress and, as far as anyone knows, only held one car for a short time and a solitary hand-driven lawn-mower was the only longstanding resident ever to grace the interior of this magnificent garage.

Louie Fioravanti had worked for the Boyce and Lazarus Glove Company for over a year and, in the summers, he would take the leather from the first floor to the second and third, where it was to be graded and up to the top floor which housed the glove-cutters. During the warm weather, Louie would step out of the windows and use the fire-escape to reach the various floors. One sunny summer day, Louie was returning leather from the fourth floor and stepped out, as was his custom, onto what he thought was the fire-escape. He was not aware that it had been taken apart to be repaired and repainted and he fell four floors down to the ground below. It appeared that the only thing which saved his life was the large bundle of leather which he was carrying at the time and on top of which he landed, breaking his fall and saving his life. However, his left arm was severely damaged and would be the source of pain for him for the rest of his life. At the time, it was almost impossible to find a doctor who could successfully help Louie with his arm. Although he never lost the use of it, many operations were performed, and the arm was never completely healed. After this painful episode, his mother, Donida would always refer to Louie as "disfortunata, the unfortunate one". Young Bill Fioravanti would often hear his mother crying out in Sicilian dialect, about the "disfortunata", and consequently would come to resent and hate that phrase and would subsequently never have a good relationship with his brother.

As the year was coming to an end, Bill Fioravanti learned that property at the nearby resort area of Caroga Lake was off limits to Italians and Jews and he was sufficiently inflamed by this that he determined to prove that he could buy land in that area. He was proved right and bought a piece of land which consisted of about one and a half acres at the top of a roadway called Scott Road from a Mr. Lake. If Bill had attempted to buy land located a mile or so north of Scott Road, he would have run into a solid wall of obstacles. In all deeds of land at the time it was clearly stated that no particles of this land were ever to be sold to either Jews or Italians. Bill had been hoodwinked but, once again, the Master builder, George Cali, would be called upon to construct another edifice that people would talk about for years to come.

Chapter 29: The Barn Burners

A year before William Faulkner's short story, "The Barn Burners", appeared in Harper's Magazine, six Sicilians were being tried for arson in a country court-house in Fonda, New York, which is a small rail-road town in Montgomery County, and which is also the county seat. The fact that these six men, which included two boys, were being tried in Montgomery County would seem strange as they were all from Johnstown, New York, which is in Fulton County. As it turned out, they were being tried there because of circumstances which had provoked the situation, and the reason for this will become clear very soon.

Out of feelings of revenge, hate, and a total lack of success in their hopeless lives, the Faulkner Barn Burners set fires and terrorized all of Mississippi. However, the Sicilians who burned down barns, motels and small useless businesses in the New York Counties of Fulton, Montgomery and Hamilton were servicing the property owners. They were like a band of "merry men" who offered this unusual service during a time when the Great Depression was bearing down very hard on many people in America. The unfortunate problem which grew out of their actions was that, although the customers were usually satisfied, the insurance companies, who had to pay out large sums of money, were not. The animosity which grew with the insurance companies led them to develop a solution that would bring an end to this band of self-servers and, in June, 1938, the band of "merry men" was ultimately disbanded and finally brought to justice.

Who were these men and how did they find themselves in such an unusual line of work? In order to answer this question, one has to return to the first decade of the twentieth century and to Salvatore (Sam) Valentino's early days in Johnstown. At this point in time, the Johnstown buildings were primarily old wooden structures which were like natural fire hazards and which were constantly catching on fire and providing constant activity for firemen. On a warm night around 1918, Sam Valentino was on his way home from the local Waterway Bar and happened to pass a house that was going up in flames on Water Street. Sam stood along with a crowd of people who were watching the blaze since fires at that time were main events and always drew many onlookers. As the flames engulfed the building, Sam overheard some of the people talking to each other and saying how the owner of the house would be getting a large settlement from the insurance company. He had no idea at the time what insurance even was, but he wasted no time in finding out and thus into his nefarious mind was the creation of a new breed of barn-burners. Although Sam's idea was not to reach fruition until almost ten years later, the seeds were already firmly planted in his brain as to what would eventually become a very profitable and long tenure of income.

It was not unusual in the early decades of the twentieth century America to find men spending their spare time hanging around barber shops just like they were in the habit of standing around the cracker barrel to discuss politics, exchange small talk and catch up on the local gossip. Mr. Tom Lizio's shop happened to be one of the more popular places where men gathered, and Sam Valentino was part of the regular group who frequented the Lizio store.

Sometime late in 1928, Tom Lizio happened to mention that a regular customer had brought up the fact that one of his superiors, from a Caroga Lake Motel where he worked, had complained that the motel was draining his pocketbook and that he wished it would burn to the ground so that he could collect insurance and be rid of it for once and for all. Sam Valentino happened to be there that day and, after most of the men had left, he stayed behind to discuss with Tom what he had just heard. It had been ten years since Sam had watched the fire on Water Street, but he had never forgotten it and the possibilities which flames promised. From his early time in Sicily, Sam still had the expertise of starting and stopping fires, and he could never erase the memories of his time spent in the Sicilian mines of Enna. With these thoughts whirling through his head, Sam approached Tom with the outrageous idea of offering services to the motel owner and getting a fee for effort. This course of action was agreed upon between the two men and now came the problem of how to set all in motion.

By some means, Tom stealthily contacted the disgruntled motel owner and a fee for services was later agreed upon. This first fire was to ignite the beginning flames of the Fulton County Barn Burners, yet the two men had together realized at this point that more than just two men would be needed if the venture was to succeed. After much meshing of ideas, they decided who they hoped would be reliable members of their newly formed band. Tom quickly recruited his youngest and favorite son who was known as Tom Junior and who was still a minor. His father was confident that, should things go awry, because of his youthful age, little or nothing could happen to his son as far as the law was concerned. The next new band member whom they recruited was to be Carmelo Rotella who rented a room above Tom's old warehouse at the back of the property. Little is known about the history of Carmelo and how he arrived in Johnstown, and he seemed to disappear from sight when the band's work eventually tumbled down. The fourth member was Carmelo Carminiti who was known locally as the "renegade". He had unending courage and daring so badly needed by the group if endeavors were to succeed, and with the special skills of each other member, there would indeed be many assignments in the next ten years which were successfully completed.

With their first assignment being set to take place in the middle of the night, the band headed for Caroga Lake and drove towards the motel. Tom Junior was assigned as driver and drove on all subsequent assignments except for the fateful night in the future when things were brought to a grinding halt. Armed with coal oil, kerosene, and Sam Valentino's knowledge and experience of fires, their first act of arson was begun. Sam took leadership and gave out directions which all the men eagerly followed. Seemingly within seconds, the entire motel was ablaze after a very loud, explosive, boom. By the time this happened, Tom Jr. had already driven the car half way back to Johnstown. Sam had such cunning and knowledge as to exactly ignite a blaze so that the men would be far from the burning structure by the time the fire was discovered. His superior skill always seemed to work so that the band of Merry Men always had an air-tight alibi. They were never seen in the vicinity of the crime.

Tom Senior took care of the finances and later called on the motel owner for payment of the well performed services. The money was good and plentiful to be shared between the four men and, even though young Tom only received what his father gave him, all band members were satisfied.

Like all good things, word spread quickly about the newly formed organization and soon work started to pour into the group like a flood. Since the financial situation was not very good in the three counties of Fulton, Montgomery and Hamilton, the resort areas were consequently suffering the most and it was in those three counties that Tom and Sam would make most of the fortune that they would soon accumulate.

Although at this time, things were bad in many other American locations, the Johnstown Flats were flourishing. The majority of properties on Cayadutta and Burton Streets were well cared for and nicely painted and houses were surrounded by beautiful lawns and attractive shrubbery. Many new people had established themselves in the area. Mrs. Greco and her family, Jenny, Sam and Tony, had taken residence on the north-west corners of Cayadutta and Burton Streets.

An old lady, Mrs. Greco, who was called the "Queen of Cayadutta" owned a big house and created a convenience store in a small building next to her house. Her husband never made an appearance and no-one knew if he even existed so, seemingly on her own, she set up shop where she sold bread, pasta and penny candy.   Her biggest and most popular commodity, however, was loaning money to young men such as Bill Fioravanti Jr., Frank Ruggeri, and others from the Flats. Her money-lending was so appreciated that all the young men in particular were crazy about her even though she dressed in shabby old clothes and never bothered about her appearance. Her kind spirit and motherly nature made her into a sort of legend in the following years.

Another resident, Benjamino Melita, took his profits from boot-legging and bought the buildings on the west corner of Cayadutta Street where it intersected with State Street. He owned a total of six buildings which began with the last house on Cayadutta, and then two more houses behind. He owned three more decidedly slummy houses on West State Street. Benjamino rented some of these houses and converted one of them, for his own use, into a liquor store and another into a grocery shop. He also rented the apartments above the stores, so he was making a lot of money even without his thriving bootlegging business.

Mr. Paul Oliver, who was on the opposite corner from Mr. Melita, was also experiencing gradual and profitable growth. He was wise in his application of the Barn Burners' methods. It seemed that every time he needed to expand, a fire would take place in his store and this would usually occur on a Sunday. His family lived upstairs and they would all come down the outside stair-case in the early morning, in full view of all the neighbors and wearing their sleeping gowns. They were like a gaggle of geese as they descended the staircase. Soon after the fire, Mr. Oliver's store would become newer and much larger than the one before.

Sam Valentino had also been making wise financial investments. He bought all the land on the west side of Aiken Street which stretched from John Street to Hall Avenue, and he would step by step own all the land from the beginning of Hall Avenue until he owned half of the entire street. Mr. Oliver built a great brick house on this avenue, but he first had to buy the land from Sam Valentino. Tom Lizio would invest his money in improving his property and buying land in the Adirondack Mountains where he was making most of his income. He also became a wise money-lender and profited greatly with the interest he charged on his loans. Word spread very quickly in the neighborhoods about the fires and the "Merry Men" and of the increasing fortunes of many who readily used the special services.

At the time of all this bustling activity, the New York State troopers knew who these arsonists were but could prove nothing, and they could find no proof of materials used to start the fires. Tom Lizio had a subterranean room beneath his huge warehouse and it was there that the special volatile materials were stored and hidden. Years passed and the frustrated troopers finally figured out a plan that would curb the Merry Men's rampage which had been going on for such a long time.

The insurance companies, who were endlessly paying out claims for the burned out buildings, were exerting pressure and finally provided impetus to solve the dilemma of proof for what seemed like an insoluble problem. In consolidating a plan of action, the troopers decided to exploit and employ Tom Lizio's weakness; his good heart. Like a Good Samaritan, Tom, as the troopers knew, would never turn away a poor, hungry soul who approached him for shelter and food. Little did Tom know that, through his open heart and welcoming nature, he was about to help the one poor soul who would bring him and his band to its painful, devastating and totally unexpected demise.

Chapter 30: Welcome Intruder

During the latter part of the nineteenth century, when the railroads were weaving their iron web all over America, they created what became known as railroad hotels. In Johnstown, the American Hotel in the Flats was one of them. It was situated thirty feet from the railroad tracks which crossed West State Street, just a hundred feet across from Tom Lizio's property. This hotel was one of those buildings that had been abandoned or built when the railroads were spreading into areas called spurs. As the owners left the structures, the railroad or enterprising people grabbed the buildings and turned them into hotels and housing for the railroad workers.

The Johnstown American Hotel served the same function as did most of these so-called hotels in the country. Most of these buildings were clap-board and had not seen a coat of paint since their inception. Eventually, they became ugly run-down edifices which cluttered and spoiled the landscape. It was of no surprise that they primarily housed the poor and disenfranchised of most communities. They became what were to be known as flop-houses. The American Hotel perfectly fit this description and catered to the lowest of the low. The Sicilian townsfolk did not very often venture into this environment as it was considered dangerous and beneath their dignity.

Pietro Longo, who had been living in the American Hotel for four days, was completely destitute. He was working as a swamper in a bar which was located directly off West State Street, and it is was easy to see the bar activity as one passed by. Pietro knew that he needed to find a way to make a decent living or his end was uncertain. Little was known about Pietro Longo except that he had arrived at the Railway Express Office of the F.J. and G. Railroad which was located on a strip of land that stretched from West State Street to West Main all along the railway tracks. Pietro's story was that he had fallen asleep in a box car, and that when it was redirected to

Johnstown, he was awakened by the yard boss at the Railway Express Building. His own version of how he arrived in Johnstown included catching freight trains that would take him to California. His story seemed very believable as, all over America young men and some boys were trying to get out west where it was told that golden opportunities awaited them all.

Many things in life are not always as they seem to be. Pietro Longo gave the appearance of a poor, shabbily dressed man who was slight of body and who needed a good haircut and a clean shave. He looked about twenty-three years old, but in reality, was closer to thirty. This unfamiliar man, who would become the Intruder, was indeed an undercover state trooper and had been assigned to infiltrate the Barn Burners. After many years of failure, the troopers had, they thought, finally figured out a way to flush out the Barn Burners and put an end to their reign.

It was a wet, cold late April day and Pietro was standing outside the bar of the American Hotel smoking the remains of a cigarette, since he ostensibly could not afford to buy a regular pack of smokes. He was standing there with a particular purpose in mind. He knew that Tom Lizio daily passed by and Pietro planned to finally make his move on the gang. Exactly as he figured, Tom Lizio came strolling by and, on this occasion, Pietro stopped Tom and asked him if he could use him in his store as a general helper. Tom saw what he deemed to be a poor boy in rags and in need of food and better shelter than the hotel could offer. After thinking for a moment, he unwittingly told the Intruder to be at his store at about five p.m. that same day and they would discuss his future. Pietro knew that at last he was going to enter the domain which had eluded the troopers for so long.

A clock hung over the bar in the America Hotel. It had a cracked glass covering its face and one had to twist one's head in a certain way to tell the exact time. Pietro had been twisting his head for close to an hour in anticipation for his five o' clock meeting with Tom Lizio. With one last twist of the head, he could see that the time was five minutes to five and at last he would be able to finally set in motion the events that brought about the end of the Barn Burners' activities.

Pietro found Tom waiting for him in the barber shop and commenced his plea for assistance. He told Tom that he had encountered some problem in a town near Albany and was trying to leave the state before he found himself in serious trouble. Being a man of big heart, Tom was sympathetic to the young man's entreaties and saw what he believed to be a person possessed of special qualities and agreed to have Pietro work for him and provide shelter and food. However, Tom insisted that the young man should immediately clean himself up with a shave and a good haircut. With much trepidation, Pietro sat in the barber's chair and Tom lathered him up for a shave. Pietro knew that, if for any chance Tom suspected that the young man was an undercover trooper, his throat could be cut in the blink of an eye. There are times in life when one has to go with one's inner instincts and, for Pietro, the time had come. After trusting his own instincts, the shave and haircut were safely concluded and he breathed a sigh of relief and looked forward, with relish, to the wonderful meal, about which he had heard, that Josephine Lizio had prepared for the evening's welcome.

When the complete family of wife and six children had gathered for the meal, Tom Sr. introduced Pietro as their new family member. Since the Intruder knew that it is usually safest to extract information from the youngest member of a group or family Pietro thought that he would eventually try to become very close to Tom Jr. who would readily reveal the Barn Burners' plans. Immediately, all the Lizio family seemed to accept Pietro and made him feel that he had been born to their clan. A bed was set up in the room occupied by Tom Jr. and soon the two would engage in much conversation which especially concerned the exciting exploits of the Barn Burners. Tom Jr. spewed out information that would bury his father and save his brother Sam who had little or nothing to do with the nefarious machinations of his father and his merry band. However, as circumstances would have it, in the final analysis, his brother Sam would be part of the troopers' final solution. It was told to Pietro by Tom Jr. that none of the other family members knew anything of the band's activities and had nothing to do with their actions. In garnering all this information, Pietro would help some of the band and family members, while he would hurt others.

Things were proceeding with such perfection that Pietro could hardly believe it. He had been given orders that, once he had gained the complete confidence of the family, he was to find a way to become a member of the band of merry men. Through his growing close relationship with Tom Jr., he convinced the young Lizio that he would be a helpful part of the group and, after much deliberating, Tom Sr. and Sam Valentino agreed to bring Pietro into their gang. A new contract was at hand and in the middle of May it would be D-day.

Life is not always as simple as black and white or good and bad. It is more about the shifting areas of shades of grey.

Pietro was finding that he had sympathies for the Lizio family that had taken a chance on a drifter who just happened to be passing by. Their kindness and the children's acceptance of him were both affecting his conscience. At night he found himself tossing and turning as he thought of the terrible blow that he would deliver to fell this good man and his family. If he had been just been betraying the Barn Burners he would have felt no pangs of guilt but to hurt the rest of the family was bringing him terrible grief.

At last the day arrived for the band to complete their latest contract. Tom Jr. would stay at home and Pietro would drive in his place. The merry men and their new driver headed north to a small motel near Speculator which was deserted since its owner had lost a considerable amount of money trying to maintain it during the terrible depression that was strangling much of the country. Upon their arrival, the gang set about doing what they usually did, and Pietro saw firsthand how all was accomplished. Later he would use these observations to avoid a long drawn-out state trial. With the task complete, the men took off in their usual fashion and were far away when the motel burned to the ground.

What a revelation all this was to Pietro as he accumulated the information which was needed to bring all the men to justice! The big question to him was when and how to expose them. It was late May and, knowing that he could not last much longer as the Intruder, he was fully aware that he would have to act very soon. One day before the end of the month, Pietro slipped away and contacted the troop commander. Together these two troopers plotted the next move. The plan was that Pietro would casually mention to Tom Sr. that he had a friend who might be of some use to the band. Tom took the bait and, before one knew it, Pietro made arrangements for that friend to come and make a proposal to Tom Sr. and to Sam Valentino. There was a sense of urgency as Pietro thought that, if he did not act quickly, some members of the gang might vanish and then the arrest would be incomplete.

Dom Franchi was a formidable looking man, and when he met the two leaders of the merry men, they were impressed. He outlined a job that was to take place in a small rural town called Fort Plain which was west of the Mohawk River with the railway running through. The men were to burn down a barn which was owned by a small farmer who had fallen on bad times. The date for the burning was set for June 4th, 1938, and this would be a day to go down in infamy for this small group of not to be so merry men.

When June 4th arrived, all were prepared to depart for Fort Plain. There was, however, a hitch in their plan since Tom Jr., was ill with the flu and the driving was delegated to his brother Sam. He vehemently protested, but was overruled by his father and thus was placed in what would become a precarious position. Finally, with Sam as the driver, and with an extra man, the merry men set off.

Everything seemed normal as the band arrived at the site of the barn. Sam Valentino gave out instructions to his men who began preparing to set the blaze that would demolish the barn. No sooner that all was in place, from out of the barn and from the surrounding land, there appeared ten men in trooper's uniforms. They immediately set about arresting all the merry men who were subsequently taken to the trooper barracks in Montgomery County where they were subsequently interrogated and badly beaten. Tom Sr. and Sam Valentino were so harshly treated that they were almost killed. Rotella and Carminiti, members of the band, were also beaten but not as harshly as the other two. Sam was not hit but was incarcerated for the next four days. Although Tom Jr. was not present, Pietro had provided the troopers with all the necessary information to indict him. There would be leniency for Sam who had never participated in any of the arsonist activities.

It turned out that Judge Crangle, who presided over the sentencing, was fair and flexible in his judgment of the men. Harold Ward, who was the public defender for Tom Sr., Tom Jr., Sam Lizio, Carmelo Rotella, and Carmelo Carminiti, argued that these men could not have a fair trial because they were Italian-Americans. The district attorney protested this line of thinking and appealed to Judge Crangle to ignore the plea and mete out the harshest punishments under the law. However, it is to be believed that, being influenced by the famous Sacco and Vanzetti trial in which Judge Thayer had so blatantly discounted evidence and support from famous people such as Einstein and Edna Saint Vincent Millay, and other notable dignitaries, Judge Crangle was more objective in his final verdicts. Sam Valentino, as was usually the case, acted smarter than the rest of the band, and hired two lawyers, Fayette and Mayer to represent him and won just a short term in prison as opposed to Tom Sr.

It was finally agreed, when all were arraigned, that they would plead guilty and request lesser sentences. Sam Lizio was fined and given a one year suspended sentence in the

Onondaga Penitentiary where Carmelo Carminiti, Carmelo Rotella and Salvatore (Sam) Valentino also were ordered to go together with pay fines.   Tom Jr. was given a one year suspended sentence to the Elmira Reformatory.   The worst punishment was placed on the head of Tom Lizio Sr. since he was the proclaimed leader of the group and had planned most of the fires. He was ordered to spend not less than five or more than ten years in the Danamora Prison.

Since all the band members had made plea bargains, there was no trial and this was the end of a reign of men who not only profited greatly themselves but helped others to likewise profit. On the Johnstown Flats residents were shocked and extremely distressed over the sentence that Tom Sr. had received. For years to come they would fester over what had happened to this "Good Samaritan" who to them had been such a generous supporter and now sadly gone for such a long time.

In later years after he was released, it is sad to note that Tom Sr. lost both of his legs to diabetes and many attributed his failing health to the awful beatings which he had received from the Montgomery County troopers at the time of his arrest. There was so much sympathy for Tom Sr. and, when he finally died, a box of his, full of I O U's for people whom he had helped and supported in his Glory Days, was found. Donida Fioravanti, along with so many other local residents would forever claim that taking Tom Sr.'s heartful, welcoming nature and his ultimate tragic end as an example for all to see, no-one should ever, ever, make friends with a cop!

Chapter 31: Cousin Joe

Night was falling on New York City as the Conte
Biancomano ship glided into New York Harbor. Giuseppe
Andrea Andreana could barely see the magnificent Manhattan
skyline as the darkness began to engulf the city. He was full of
anxiety and wonder as he stood on the deck, preparing to
disembark from the ship that he felt had carried him to safety
and to a" Brave New World". It was difficult for Giuseppe to
see if he could recognize anyone who might look like his uncle
Bill Fioravanti and, after his feet touched solid ground, he
thought he saw someone who resembled him. He was correct
and soon found himself in the embrace of Don Guglielmo
(Bill) Fioravanti. The uncle addressed his new nephew as
"Joe", and Joe referred to Bill as "Zio", which in Italian means
"uncle". In order for Joe to have someone near his age to talk
to and who could speak Italian, Bill had brought along his
oldest daughter, Maria.

When everything was cleared with customs, fees, etc.,
they all headed for Grand Central Station to catch a train for
Fonda. Although Joe could not see much of the city as it was
in complete darkness at this time, he could, however, see the
beautiful interior of the station which was the new and final
one which would survive into the twenty-first century and
which had lived up to all the publicity that had surrounded it
when it was first announced that a new Grand Central Station
was going to be built. Cousin Joe gazed in amazement at the
beautiful interior with its Greek columns that held up the
glorious and ornate ceiling and the spacious marble floor with
the information center sitting in its middle. This wonderful
new station was so much more ornate than the old one through
which Guglielmo and Joe Brunetto had entered so long ago in
1910. Joe found it breathtaking and imagined that, if all of
America was like this, where would it end?   Alas, poor
man. Life does not always live up to first impressions and Joe
was soon to find out that people and circumstances can alter

any situation. However, for the time being, Joe would bask in this euphoric state as long as possible.

As the three Sicilians boarded the Pullman car that would carry them to Fonda and then to Johnstown, all Joe could only think of was that he was free at last. As a youth he had endured intense hardships that were usually suffered by adults. During the years in the orphanage he had found ways to earn meager amounts of money in order to survive, and he kept himself in physical shape by engaging in gymnastics. A brighter future was all Joe could imagine on this day of May 4, 1931 and all the lessons which he had learned from a previous rough and difficult life would mold this man into what many people would refer to as "one of God's children". Of course, there was no way for Joe to realize what lay ahead for him with Donida Fioravanti.

The train took its usual path along the beautiful Hudson Valley and then into the Mohawk Valley and finally arrived in Fonda where all the family members took the trolley to Johnstown. It was late and dark upon their arrival at 22, Cayadutta Street which was the birthplace of Joe and the Fioravanti boys. Donida was awake and as cordial as was possible for her when she greeted them at the door. After such a long trip and, not needing food as the weary travelers had eaten on the way, Joe was shown where he could sleep. Everyone in the family slept upstairs and there were plenty of rooms and lots of space and a bathroom so that no-one had to go down the back stairs during the night. Joe washed up, bid all good night, hit the bed, and left the world for a good seven hours.

When Joe awakened the following morning, he was greeted with a special breakfast, which in the Fioravanti household as in most Sicilian homes, was usually a bowl of warm milk and bread. This morning, however, as a welcoming meal for Joe and because this was a very special time, all were treated to eggs, toast, and honey. Mary Ruggeri would often mention to others that all that could be afforded at her home was a bowl of coffee and bread since milk was a far too expensive drink for her father to buy. Although these peasant breakfasts do not now seem very nutritious, the young Sicilians grew up strong and healthy.

After Joe had finished his meal and had met all the family, he felt very good about his situation. The boys, Bill Jr. and Louie were kind and caring to their cousin as were Mary and Josephine and little Mary Ruggeri who had run over early to the Fioravanti house to meet this new family member. In all the years that Joe and his cousins lived in Johnstown and Gloversville, the Fioravanti family only spoke with the highest regard for their cousin Joe. In the late part of Joe's life, he showed extreme kindness and compassion especially for his cousin Mary, and everyone who saw this affection which Joe and even his wife Teresa exhibited towards their cousin, was extremely impressed.

Bill Sr. had decided to take Joe on a tour of the neighborhood and, as Bill opened the front door and sunlight poured into the hallway, Joe blinked for a minute and then stepped out into the verdant and what appeared to be a bucolic setting. As they ambled along Cayadutta Street and occasionally stopped to talk to various people, all Joe could think about was how these Sicilians had been transplanted into what appeared to be a Garden of Eden. Everyone spoke Sicilian dialect and expressed Sicilian ways in their manners and demeanor, and Joe was stunned by this and felt that he had come to his home where he was meant to live and thrive. However, he had absolutely no idea of what Donida Fioravanti had planned for his beginnings in the New World.

At first Joe rested and then explored the neighborhood, which he found to be an almost familiar environment, where all he had to do was step in knowing that he was surrounded by his own people. This gave him a sense of exaltation and confidence. Young people need to feel secure and safe in new places, and Joe's sense of all this would help him to survive in the year that lay ahead. In the beginning, Donida's demands on Cousin Joe were meager to say the least. He was asked to do chores such as take out the garbage or help weed the garden and these demands were not very much considering all the attention he was receiving. The food was wonderful, the accommodations were better than average, and he was living in the most beautiful house in the neighborhood. Sometimes Joe brought water or coffee to Mr. Cali who was building the large preposterous garage at the back of the house which would never hold an automobile but would eventually house that small hand lawn-mower.

Things had begun to change in the Fioravanti household after Louie fell out of the fourth-floor window at the Boyce and Lazarus Glove Company. Donida was constantly beside herself as she cared and doted over Louie whose wounds would not heal for years after the fall. She became harder and more demanding of Joe who was ordered to remove the ashes from the cellar furnace and to help with cleaning, whereas his cousins, Bill Jr. and Louie never did anything around the house and contributed even less in terms of financial assistance. It now seemed to Joe that the sky was falling on him and he once again got the feeling that he had when he was an inmate back at the orphanage in Sicily.

Don Guglielmo and Mike Mazzaro most likely did not notice what was transpiring with Joe and the children paid even less attention. Perhaps Donida's malicious treatment of her nephew was due to constantly worrying about her son, Louie. When it came to her sons, she was obsessive and may have questioned to herself why it was her son and not Joe who was writhing in pain. No-one will ever know her motives but whatever they were, Joe was the direct object of her disdain.

At this time, the inhabitants in Gloversville were predominantly Italians from Naples, but there was one Sicilian resident there, a Mr. DiStefano, whom Bill Fioravanti knew well and who owned a produce business on the corner of South Main Street and Woodside Avenue in Gloversville. The

DiStefano's lived next door to the business and had easy access to their work-place. At the time, this was

not an uncommon thing as even big industrialists often lived near to or next to their mills and factories. Bill Sr. used to visit Mr. DiStefano from time to time and usually took Bill Jr. and his sister, Mary and now started to take along Joe Andreana as well. It was from these visits that Joe became friendly with the DiStefano family.

Joe had not only been doing most of the chores at 22, Cayadutta Street but was also working part-time for Denkert's Sporting Goods alongside his cousins, Mary and Josephine. It was at this time that one day, when he arrived home from his job, he was confronted with a request which would catapult him out of the house and turn him into a man overnight.

A real Sicilian thing was about to occur and it would indeed shock Joe. Josephine Fioravanti, the younger daughter, was a wonderful, loving lady but not very attractive to young men. Her mother, Donida, realized that Josephine had little chance of ever becoming a bride, so it came into her mind that she should marry her first cousin, Joe Andreana. In her own thoughts, Donida felt that since they had taken him in as a son, Joe owed that favor to her and to his uncle. However, as was previously mentioned, he was gifted with a native intelligence and knew the possible consequences of such a marriage. He mumbled a few words in response to Donida's suggestion to the effect that he would think about the idea, but he knew that there was nothing that he really had to think about and quickly prepared to make his escape from 22, Cayadutta Street. Facing the problem as to where he would flee, Joe decided to approach Mr. DiStefano in Gloversville, as it always appeared to him that he was well-liked by the old man. The year was 1932, and late in the night Joe stole away and made for the DiStefano's to plead for assistance. For some reason, Mr. DiStefano complied and agreed to give Joe sanctuary. He would be allowed to live in the back room of the store and could help out with the produce business. Giuseppe Andrea

Andreana was on his way to becoming an independent man and would remain that way for the rest of his life.

Bill Fioravanti finally figured out where his nephew Joe was, and as was his way, would be prepared to forgive Joe when he made the trip to see him in Gloversville and ask him to return to Johnstown, but Joe was adamant that he would stay in Gloversville with the DiStefano's. Feeling upset at Joe's decision, Bill gave his blessings to his nephew and wished him well and would, nevertheless from this time, always consider Joe to be an important part of the family. The Fioravanti children also felt no ill-will or hard feelings towards their cousin when he decided to stay in Gloversville but, of course, no-one was sure as to how Donida Fioravanti really felt, but she never dared to go against the decisions of her husband or of Mike Mazzaro.

Joe worked hard and became an apprentice in one of the Gloversville glove shops eventually becoming a glove-cutter and making a decent living. He also attended night school and learned to read and write the English language. Joe was an up-and- comer and readily made friends with the young men of Gloversville. They would all go together to dances and look for fun and girls. Caroga Lake, a resort area about nineteen miles from Gloversville, would sponsor dances during the summer week-ends. It was at one of these dances that Joe encountered a young girl with whom he would fall in love and be devoted to for his entire life to come. Her name was Teresa DiDonato and she captured Joe's heart. After dating for a couple of years, the two were married on August 24, 1935. Bill Fioravanti Sr. and Donida did not attend the wedding, but Bill Jr. and Louie were present on this occasion. It was not unusual for one or the other not to attend if a Sicilian was marrying a Neapolitan. Italians! What can you say? Together, Joe and Teresa would have two children and, as Teresa was such a lovely woman, the couple would complement each other for their entire married life.

Giuseppe Andrea Andreana, now known as Joe, would be the last offspring still standing of the two brothers who had come so long ago from Castelmola, Sicily. Joe would pass in 2007, after having suffered through such pain and torture of his childhood and early youth, all the way through this he had lived what can only be truly described as an exemplary life.

Chapter 32: Events and the Wedding

During the 1930's there never was a shortage of intrigue or activities at 22, Cayadutta Street. Guglielmo had had the old barn burned down and would wrestle with his conscience over that for many a year. Cousin Joe had arrived and fled under unusual circumstances. Louie had fallen out of a fourth floor window and lived. For the Fioravanti family, the thirties had started off with a bang and would continue exploding for practically the entire decade. Over a tender notion that came to Mike Mazzaro, he would have to deal delicately with Donida.

Bill Fioravanti and Michael Mazzaro would have many arguments over the man known as Il Duce or Mussolini. Bill took the peasant's point of view that, due to Mussolini's insistence, trains were now punctual for the first time since their inception as a mode of transport in Italy, and education now existed for all people. Mike, on the other hand, argued from an aristocrat's standpoint and claimed that the Fascists were brutal and tyrannical in the way they instituted the laws. The two men's exchanges were heated but never reached a point where there would be constant lingering animosity. Theirs was a divine friendship in which the two disagreed on many things but they still admired and cared unconditionally for each other.

Donida always respected the demands and wishes of both Bill Sr. and Michael Mazzaro, except for a special request that came to her attention. She would not allow animals of any kind into her house and Mike had a notion that he would like to own some dogs. After discussing his desire with Bill, both men agreed that asking Donida for this special request would be like banging one's head against the wall, and so Mike came up with a solution that he hoped would satisfy all the parties concerned. He would build a dog house in the back yard. However, the one he subsequently built was not the ordinary run-of-the-mill dog house. It was high enough for a grown man to stand straight up without bending over, and it was more like a miniature shed with a pot-bellied stove and warm blankets so that the dogs would not freeze in the cold winter months. After completing the building, Mike acquired two dogs to occupy it. The first dog was a black Irish setter called Sylvia whose name came from Errol Flynn's dog in the movie, "The Green Light". The other dog was a retired greyhound called Flash. No two dogs ever had a better and longer quality of life than those two dogs. Even Donida became genuinely attached to them.

In Johnstown, pollution was an ever-increasing problem, especially for the people in the Flats. The Cayadutta Creek had become worse than ever and was a breeding place for mice and rats. The vermin would come up from the creek bed and invade the houses along Cayadutta Street. Donida came up with her own solution to that problem. The back of the 22, Cayadutta Street housed a large semi-detached porch and Donida would soon turn it into a home for seven to ten cats which would patrol the complete property and make sure that no rodents would ever enter the home of Don Guglielmo Fioravanti. Her plan worked very well since no mice or rats were ever to be seen inside the house. People called the cats" Italians" because Donida always fed them elbow pasta, meatballs and a small amount of milk. All the cats seemed to be very contented and multiplied until there probably were as many as twelve to thirteen cats in total. However, true to form, no cat was ever allowed inside but in the summer months, when the back porch screen door was open, a strong smell of Lysol and other disinfectants pervaded the house. Even with so many cats, the peasant woman from Castelmola, Sicily would maintain an ultra-clean and sanitary environment. Donida was immaculately clean until the day she died and worked all her life to maintain a high standard of cleanliness.

Mary and Josephine Fioravanti had grown up and were now young ladies in their mid-twenties. However, there was

nothing enviable about their lives. They worked all day at
Denkert's Sporting Goods Factory, and after this they were
enslaved by their mother who had them constantly cleaning,
dusting, and washing clothes when they came home. Mary
was delegated to washing windows and throughout the rest of
her life, after Donida's passing, she would never want to clean
or have anything to do with windows. The younger Josephine
took most of the brunt of Donida's wrath which was fairly
prevalent towards her daughters. She was beaten and
constantly belittled. After Josephine's premature death in the
early forties, Donida would guiltily moan and carry on for
many years about her deceased daughter.

The only compensation that the two daughters seemed to
have was that they were always dressed in very decent clothes
and kept up a good personal appearance. They had no
gentlemen callers and their social life was restricted to
activities which took place in the church hall directly opposite
22, Cayadutta Street. The church pastor was Father Burke who
was of Irish heritage and beloved by most of the Sicilian
parishioners. He held mass in the church hall because the
Immaculate Conception Church had burned down a few years
prior to his arrival. His assistant pastor was a very handsome
Father Lohengrin who Louie Fioravanti would take along
when he went gambling and frequenting various brothels.
Mary Fioravanti was involved in the church Rosary Society
which most Catholic churches formed at the time. These
Rosary Societies had many members and would meet every
week in different parishioners' homes. Much to Donida's
chagrin, since Don Guglielmo and Mike Mazzaro approved of
the society and its meetings, Mary was allowed to take her
turn and have her church meetings in the front parlor, which
in Donida's view, should only be used for special visitors
and for funerals. Italian festivals were another big part of the
girls' meager social life, but they were only held for two weeks
once a year during the summer months. However, as joyless
and bleak as their lives were, Mary was the sister who would

eventually survive all the tribulation, get to see the world, fall in love, learn how to speak and write in Italian, and gain an enormous amount of knowledge. It just took a lifetime.

Constantino (Louie) had been healing since his fall and was changing his life around. He had experienced a falling out with Joe Brunetto Jr. about dividing stolen goods from Sponables Store. Louie claimed that Joe never paid him his share and consequently never spoke to him again for the rest of his life. Nevertheless, he did eventually find his true vocation and for the rest of his life would be devoted to it. He was no longer a petty thief and a burglar. He had graduated from that line of business and had stepped out into the sophisticated world of the eternal gambler.

As an apprentice gambler, Louie was now meeting a better class of people such as Bucky O'Connor who ran most of the gambling in Johnstown. Mr. O'Connor was an affable man who was not only involved in local betting but who also basically ran the entire political side of the Johnstown community. His second-in-command man was a Slovak named Tanzer Komornik who just happened to be the brother of the Sergeant of the Johnstown Police department. Tanzer was also an affable, nice man and not at all like his brother, the police officer. A very important fact concerning Bucky O'Connor was that, no matter how much a man lost at the gambling table, if he was a family man, Bucky would never let him leave the gaming room without some money. He was a sincerely, good man who, throughout his life, lent his experience and influence to help many Johnstown people. Unlike so many of his fellow countrymen, this Irishman showed no prejudice towards any other ethnic group in the community. He would eventually be responsible for helping Bill Fioravanti's daughter, Mary, to bring her husband to the United States from Cuba where he was in exile until certain documents could be approved. It was through Bucky O'Connor's help and power that the documents were quickly approved.

Louie Fioravanti's new found way of life caused many problems for Bill Fioravanti Sr. Whenever Louie lost games and could not pay his gambling debts, Bill or Donida would have to intervene and cover the costs or Louie was likely to have to pay in other ways. This was not Mr. O'Connor's way of conducting business but Louie liked to venture into more precarious places such as Fonda which was heavily populated with railroad workers and men who demanded immediate payments on debts. However, Louie was not deterred by threats and continued down this gambling path for many decades right up to his death.

Because there was a certain glamorous association with this sordid life, Louie became a popular figure with men and, unfortunately, with women who were mostly married. He was young and handsome and was steadily becoming more intrigued with women and them with him. Trouble constantly followed Louie since chasing women became his second worse vice and he would have to deal with this all his life. There was even talk that he was in love with Mary Ruggeri who by now had grown into a very attractive girl who was catching the eye of both Fioravanti brothers. One thing seemed to be sure; Mary Ruggeri was most certainly in love with Louie as she was mooning over him whenever he was present.

There can be no doubt that the differences between Bill Jr. and Louie were remarkable. Bill, unlike his brother, was short and stocky with curly hair. He was not as handsome as Louie, but he suffered the same desires that any young man felt irrespective of looks. Another important facet of Bill's life was that he had started to acquire a desire to find work suitable for talents which he possessed but which were not clear in his own mind. The life of many second-generation Sicilians varied as to how they looked upon themselves. Louie had no inhibitions and had tremendous self-esteem. Bill, on the other hand, would struggle all his life with low self-esteem, but his special qualities would eventually allow him to have a more than average successful life.

With the extra money that young Bill earned from a promotion at his job in the glove company where he worked, he had purchased a 1931 Buick Coupe automobile. He was tired of asking to borrow the 1929 Pierce Arrow that Don Guglielmo had purchased so many years ago. With a new job and ownership of his own car, Bill started to feel better about himself. One of his greatest attributes was his leadership abilities and these started to emerge at an early age. Leaders of men are few and far between and Bill was one of those leaders. Unfortunately, he just never really grasped what his special qualities meant.

Through his gambling, Louie made a new friend named Johnny Polatino who was big and as tough as they come. His only short-coming was one missing leg. As a young boy, Johnny lived in a house on School Street which overlooked the railroad tracks. He liked to roll down the steep bank that was just above the railroad tracks and he would play on the box cars and engines that were parked near to the Railway Express Building. One day, as he was playing by the tracks, he had not noticed that one of the engines had stoked up and was ready to move. The engine sort of jumped as it prepared to hook up with a box car. Johnny was in that box car and he was bumped off and fell under the moving train. He managed to free all of his body except for his left leg which the box car ran over and severed from his body. Even with just one leg, Johnny Polatino was a formidable foe for any man. When Johnny met Bill Jr. they became fast friends and, though he never gave up gambling, he would give his all for Bill. They would have one great adventure together and Johnny's wooden leg became an amazing sight as many of the Fioravanti family members watched him dismantle it over the years.

Bill had fallen in love with Mary Ruggeri and he knew that his competition was mainly his own brother. There was some speculation that Louie was in love with Mary, but if one knew Louie intimately, it was pretty evident that he loved most of the women who were in his life. To win the heart and hand

of Mary, Bill needed a plan. Finally he decided that the only
scheme that might work was to kidnap her and he set about
implementing his plan.   One day he showed up at the
Denkert's Sporting Goods Factory where Mary worked and
offered her a ride. He never explained how far this ride would
venture, and when she stepped into that Buick, it would be one
of the last days that she would be known as Mary Ruggeri.
Bill's plan was to take her to New York City and marry her,
and he did.

When Bill and Mary arrived in New York City, they
moved on to Brooklyn. As Mary had no intention of returning
to Johnstown after a night away with a man, they began to
search for a Justice of the Peace or a Judge who would marry
them. After stopping at a local police station, the desk officer
directed them to a country club where they could find a certain
Judge Satriano. When Bill found the judge, he was asked to
perform the ceremony. He was known as Sat, and his wife
being Rose, she acted as a sort of maid of honor and someone
whom Sat found was agreeable to be best man. Mary and Bill
were then married and the four remained life-long friends. It
is difficult to speculate as to whether Mary ever loved Bill or
vice-versa, but they would have four children and remained
together for a lifetime.

Upon their return to Johnstown, both Mary and Bill knew
that they could not show up at 22, Cayadutta Street. Donida
would be out for blood and would blame Mary for stealing her
son. Bill Sr. was not overjoyed at the wedding news since he
had hoped that Louie would marry Mary Ruggeri. As usual,
Mike Mazzaro was calm and cool and he would be the decisive
factor to bring harmony back to the Fioravanti family. Bill Jr.
and his new bride took refuge at Joe Brunetto's on Burton
Street and waited for the calm which surely would come.

Don Guglielmo went out to purchase his unique idea of
an olive branch. This was to be a new pair of women's shoes
for Mary. He started his climb up Burton Street to deliver his
peace offering. It was readily accepted by the newlyweds who

shortly thereafter left Joe Brunetto's house and headed home for 22, Cayadutta Street. The day and the year of this most unusual wedding was September 21, 1937.

Chapter 33: California

"(Get Your Kicks on) Route 66)" Those are lyrics from a composition
by a jazz musician named Bobby Troup. He wrote the song in 1946 about a magical road that stretched from Chicago to Los Angeles. It was quickly recorded by Nat King Cole and would become a national icon of jazz and popular music in the United States.

This magical road would take so many people to a place that had mythical airs about it and would lead them to the Promised Land. However, ten years before Bobby Troup wrote his up-beat version of this road, a mass migration of desperate and poverty stricken humanity hit this road. At least one hundred and fifty thousand men, women, and children were fleeing from the results of the Oklahoma, Texas Panhandle and South New Mexico great "Dust Bowl". Those sorry humans were starving and having their homes foreclosed by banks and mortgage companies. The ones who could have stayed could not plant or grow crops since all of their farms' top soil had blown away, so they left along with their neighbors. The destination for all these poor souls was California. There they had heard was work and land that could be available for small farmers if they could prove their worth. Route 66 was the path through harsh lands and arduous mountains which led to the realization of all that was left of the American Dream which had been promised to so many. So these desperate folks left in broken-down cars, trucks and with only a few dollars that could be scraped up for gas and food for survival. Despite all the hardships to be overcome on this journey, many would arrive and live to be the backbone of California.

In the East, there were others who dreamed of a new life and a new land where they could settle down and prosper. This other group was made up of men and women who were suffering the pangs of the Great Depression. Though most of this other group of people came from the large cities in the East, there also were small town men and families with their own dreams for a better and more exciting life. One such family, from the small town of Johnstown, was that of the Fioravanti's.

Bill Fioravanti Jr. was not happy with his present situation and, having inherited some of that spirit of adventure which had motivated his own father to come half way across the world while suffering unbearable conditions, had himself an urge to seek a different life. He had only been married just more than a month and he and his new wife, Mary, had been living with his parents at 22, Cayadutta Street. Bill was not happy with his job and his habitat, and he felt that he was moving at such a very slow pace with his life. Having heard about the wonderful opportunities and beautiful climate that enveloped Los Angeles, he made up his mind to take a bold leap to realize his own dream, just as his father had done so long ago. When he made this important decision, he had absolutely no idea that it would bring half the Fioravanti family out to California behind him.

Bill Jr.'s decision was not as monumental as that of his father who, from Sicily in 1910, left behind poverty, threat of disease, and absolutely no hope of a prosperous future. Bill Jr. was leaving behind a warm, comfortable bed, a new wife, a decent job which had good prospects for him, yet the spirit of adventure does not always weigh what is best and what is not. The motivator, that has moved people who accomplish and change the world, is something inside of them which can be called an intangible. Yes. To be sure, Bill Jr. had many personal problems but that intangible was not one of them. He had made up his mind and from now on would not waiver. To avoid the terrible heat of the Southwest and to miss the snow in the mountains, Bill set to leave on his trip in late October. Now all that was left for him to do was to get that 1931 Buick in good shape for the trip and to find a travelling companion.

Johnny Polatino had not been having very much luck at the gaming tables and, as he was not much of a worker, did not have a steady job. He jumped at the opportunity to go to California with Bill Jr. when he asked him and said that he would willingly scrape up enough money to pay for his share of gas and food for the trip. The best laid plans of these mice and men, citizens of Fulton County, were not feeling the pressures of the Great Depression. Some companies in Johnstown such as the Evans Company closed their doors at this time, but the Jewish Companies in Gloversville stayed open and employed a system of cutting gloves for stock and kept most of their employees working through the Great Depression. The only factor that really changed was the workers' income. Pay was reduced but it was not to a point where workers could not afford to buy food or meet their bills. Johnny Polatino did not buy into any of these alternatives and it was because of this that he showed great eagerness to go to California with Bill Jr.

Now that everything was in place, Bill Jr. explained to his new wife Mary that he would send for her as soon as he was settled in Los Angeles. Mary was always agreeable to any suggestions and would stay with Don Guglielmo, Donida, and the rest of their family until it was time for her to make the trip out west. As the third week in October approached and they prepared to leave, Bill and Johnny made sure that all was well with the car. After saying their goodbyes to their families and friends, they left on schedule. Donida was not happy with Bill's decision to leave and clearly let him know. She had her own philosophy about life and people and believed that through being kind to people in need, some good would come back to help someone in her own family. Donida lived by this code and never turned her back on the needy or downtrodden. There would be many times in her life when she would see that her code of life was being implemented on her family which was the most important thing in her life. She never varied from this thinking right up to the time of her death.

The weather from Johnstown to Chicago was cool and comfortable, and Bill and Johnny had easy sailing into the windy city. Route 66 started in Chicago and, as the two men hit the road, their adventure would really begin and they would encounter many stormy seas for the rest of the way.

The most sensitive parts of most of the cars built during the 20's and 30's were the cooling system and tires. These two factors accounted for considerable problems when the cars were driven for hours on end and for hundreds of miles without stopping.

By the time Bill and Johnny had reached St. Louis, there was a hissing outside of the Buick as if a group of rattlesnakes were riding on the hood. Bill was driving and he would drive for most of the trip. Johnny's wooden leg seemed to bother him the further they travelled. When Bill pulled the car over to a road-side diner and opened the hood, water was spraying everywhere. Now the only hope was that, when the car cooled down, they could add water and be on their way.

They were enjoying a cup of coffee and a doughnut when Johnny happened to mention that he thought the water tasted strange. The waitress, who had heard his comment, lit into Johnny and Bill calling them "No- Good -Yankees" and asked them to get out. Fortunately, at the time, a motor-cycle cop was in the diner and witnessed the entire scene. He quietly asked them to leave so as to not complicate matters any further. What had happened to Bill and Johnny was a typical scene encountered by so many people migrating westward. America is a strange place at times and many people felt that these migrants were like invaders and a lower form of life that must be watched and scrutinized for they could be dangerous. Travelling the road in bad times makes one feel either wrath or a compassion for humanity. However, one never knows which one to prepare for at the time.

Once the radiator had cooled down and returned to normal, Bill opened its cap and filled up with water, and they were on their way again. As they moved ever westward, tires blew and water had to be carried in canteens and water bags. They patched up the inner tubes and filled the radiator with fresh water as they continued westward. Before descending into the San Fernando Valley, the last mountain to be climbed is brutal, especially when driving a second-rate automobile, and Bill was praying and talking to the Buick as if she were a living, breathing object. Johnny, with his wooden leg, was also praying as he could not imagine having to get out and push the car. All Johnny's strength was from the waist up.

At last, they were approaching a small ridge that they had to conquer and from which, if they had to, they could coast down into California. What elation they felt as they were suddenly flying down the mountain into the Promised Land! Bill now knew that he could make it to Los Angeles, his final destination. It was about noon on a Friday of the first week of November, 1937 when they arrived and realized that they were flat broke and had no place to sleep. Bill drove the car behind a bill-board in downtown Los Angeles, just off Wilshire Boulevard and parked. He slumped back in the seat and fell into a peaceful sleep. Finally, he could at least find comfort in the fact that they had successfully made the trip. He would worry about food and lodging at a later time. Johnny was already sleeping and would awake to find himself in paradise.

Many hours later when the two friends awakened, they were surprised to find that they were not the only people sleeping behind that particular bill-board. Four or five other men, whom the authorities might consider derelicts or undesirables, were also occupying the same place. If the truth were known, it would manifest itself that these men were just some of the disenfranchised who were victims of the Dust Bowl and of the Great Depression. They had come from all over America to seek gold and a golden opportunity in the land of promise. For Bill and Johnny, the question was what to do next. The answer would come from an unlikely source; a professional hobo.

Fairy godmothers and godfathers have arrived in various ways over the years; some on a pumpkin, some out of a lamp, and others from the inside of a bottle. Bill's fairy Godfather would appear from behind a bill-board. As the two were standing in a state of complete bewilderment over the fact that they were homeless, penniless and hungry, out from behind the bill-board appeared a hobo, named Max, who had been watching the two young men and who he observed to be in a befuddled state. He approached them and asked what seemed to be their problem. Bill explained that they were new to Los Angeles and that they had spent all the money they had saved to get started in California. Max suggested that they all go and get a cup of coffee and something to eat. Once again, Bill remarked that they had no money, but Max just shrugged and told them not to worry. He led them to a diner near MacArthur Park and told them to order something to eat. It was very strange to expect a homeless hobo to be able to reach in his pocket and to be able to pay for three breakfasts. All Bill could think of was his mother's philosophy about helping others and being re-paid in kind. For a moment, he thought she may have been some sort of genius.

Not much was ever known about Max. He may have been a victim of the crash of '29 or another casualty of the Great Depression. Whoever he was, one thing was clear, he had intelligence and knew Los Angeles very well. Max asked what Bill and Johnny were going to do in Los Angeles and Bill simply stated that they were looking for work and for a place to live. By the time they had all finished eating Max had shown them the way to quick-start their lives in California. He found them a place to sleep in a flop house in one of the sleazier parts of downtown Los Angeles and then told them where they could find day by day work until they had secured permanent jobs. Max informed Bill to use the classified ads in the Los

Angeles Times to look for a steady job, and he paid for the flop house, wished them well, and was never seen again. Bill Fioravanti never forgot this fairy godfather, who appeared as a hobo, and he often wondered if this had been some sort of divine intervention brought on by his mother's good acts.

Working day by day kept Bill and Johnny in the flop house and there they were fed while they looked for that elusive good job which all who ventured to California expected. Finally, Bill found what he was looking for. He saw an ad in the Los Angeles Times which advertised a position with a small wool pullery in Vernon, a close suburb of Los Angeles proper and Hollywood. Bill applied for the job and, as he was from New York, was hired. His superior was a young Harvard Law graduate from Connecticut who had not taken to the law and who preferred business. His name was Henry Grossman and Bill would hold a great respect all of his life for this man.

It did not take Bill long to rise in the company and soon he was a supervisor in the grading and shipping of the wool which was pulled. He moved Johnny and himself to a small bungalow on Spaulding Avenue, just off Santa Monica Boulevard. This had two bedrooms and was large enough to accommodate Johnny, Bill and his wife, Mary, when she would finally arrive. Of course, the most important thing of all was that they were living in Hollywood, home of the stars. Now they were on their way and Bill called for Mary to come out to Hollywood. He sent her the money for the trip and Mike Mazzaro secured the tickets for her bus-ride to the Golden West.

Mary Fioravanti was packing the few meager possessions she had for her trip to California. This trip would be the greatest adventure of her life and, as it turned out, the only one. Don Guglielmo and Mike Mazzaro were preparing the car that would take Mary to the bus depot in Fonda. One would think that Mary would be pent up with anxiety and fear, but it was just the opposite. This somewhat provincial woman was excited and bursting with a feeling which was uncommon to her; that of adrenalin! All this was new to Mary and perhaps it was the anticipation of Hollywood and movie stars together with warm and sensuous climates that accounted for this new and open-minded young lady.

There was a short and very informal good-bye to her mother and father, who did not quite understand where or why Mary was going, and to her eight year old sister, Josie, who hardly knew Mary since her big sister had lived mostly with the Fioravanti's and spent little time in the Ruggeri home since she was a child. Josie and Mary would, in later years, come to love and know each other, after the Second World War, when they all worked for Bill Jr. Both Mary and Josie were very attractive girls and Josie would become an especially attractive and enticing young woman. She would be coveted by Bill Jr's boss who was a very elegant, sophisticated German Jew named Eric Firth. However, the attempted assignation never materialized and Mr. Firth would fire Josie when she later fell in love with and married a war hero, Bruno Desantis.

Upon reaching the bus depot, Don Guglielmo and Mike checked the small suit case which Mary was toting and gave her money which they thought would be sufficient for the trip to Los Angeles which used to take at least five days, providing there were no problems on the way. The long and arduous journey was fraught with all the same pitfalls that Bill Jr. and Johnny had encountered, except that this larger vehicle was carrying a much larger load. Donida had packed some food for Mary in the unlikely hope that it could last Mary until she arrived in California.

It was late in March of 1938 when this young girl, barely nineteen years of age, set off to see a new state and what eventually was to become more like a new country within a country. The snows of the east were melting and the expectation was that, as the bus moved further west, the climate would become milder. Mary slept most of the journey to Chicago and awakened in time to see the skyline as the bus approached the city limits and seemed to move along, in what seemed like no time at all. The bus moved quickly and appeared to be swept onto Route 66 and then to the yellow-brick-road towards the Golden West.

Passing through the various western states was a real eye-opener for Mary. The red clay that lined the roads in Oklahoma and the vastness of the prairies of the Texas Panhandle and New Mexico were astonishing for such a girl. She had known of these wonders from early western movies, and in a strange way, she tended to believe in the fiction created by Hollywood writers. When the bus stopped in a New Mexico town and the passengers were advised to disembark and stretch their legs, Mary would not exit as she saw Navajo Indians selling blankets and trinkets and was very frightened. She thought that, as in the movies, those red Native Americans would scalp her and, John Wayne was nowhere in sight. All would be lost, she thought. However, she did leave the bus in the Petrified Forest and in the Painted Desert of Arizona and purchased a piece of petrified wood which she treasured and kept for the rest of her life. Once the bus reached Flagstaff, Arizona, the driver announced that Los Angeles was only ten to twelve hours away.

It had been an exhilarating trip for Mary and, as the bus turned into the Los Angeles Depot, she spotted Johnny Polatino as he came limping towards the arrival place. As he was working, Bill was nowhere in sight. This would become a common occurrence for years to come in the Fioravanti home. Johnny hugged Mary, and they got into the restored 1931 Buick Coup and headed for Spaulding Avenue and Mary's new home. Johnny drove down Hollywood Boulevard so that Mary could see the great theaters such as Grauman's and the famous Roosevelt Hotel which housed so many famous stars and other celebrities. Johnny turned down La Brea to Santa Monica Boulevard, took a right turn and moved onward to the little small bungalow in the west.

This would be Mary's first real home with her new husband and she was thrilled with it. She would care for it and keep it in tip-top shape. After all, she had been trained by the greatest home-maker of all; Donida.

It is hard to imagine what transpired when Bill returned home from work and greeted his new wife. There are some things in life which will always remain a mystery because, when one finally realizes the desire to solve a mystery and ask questions, all the major characters are deceased. The one thing that was certain was that Bill, Johnny, and Mary did feel a bond together simply because they were so far away from that colonial village where they had spent their youth. Now they found themselves in a new world. And the three small-town hicks found security in each other. The only thing for which they were not prepared was a soon- to- be new arrival.

While Bill, Mary and Johnny were enjoying the warmth and wonders of Southern California, Back in Johnstown, Louie was in trouble again. He had been approached by a voluptuous lady with a proposition that they engage in a clandestine affair. Ordinarily, Louie would not only have been flattered but, most likely, would have jumped at such an unexpected request. However, this situation was very different, for Louie wanted to keep enjoying life. The young woman happened to be the wife of one of the toughest men in town and was also a celebrated boxer. For the first time in his life, Louie declined the offer and did not realize just how serious this lady's intentions were. She gave him an ultimatum: if he did not agree to her terms, she would tell her husband that they were having an affair. Louie saw no way out so, for a few months, he reveled in this adulterous liaison. Finally, just as he had foreseen, the husband learned about his wife and Louie, for whom it was now too late, realized that he was being hunted and knew that it was only a matter of time before he would be facing a confrontation in which he would not be the victor.

For the first time in his life, Constantino Louie Fioravanti was scared and sought the advice of his father and of Mike Mazzaro. Don Guglielmo thought that the only immediate solution to this problem was that Louie should leave Johnstown until things cooled down. Although Louie had no intention of leaving, after considerable persuasion by Mike and his father, it was decided that he would leave for California and go to the safety of his brother Bill Jr. It was not an easy move for Louie, but he finally agreed that it might be for the best. Mike and Don Guglielmo put together enough money for his trip and, within a few days, Louie was on a bus and on his way to California.

He arrived in California and made his way to his brother's house. As was usually the case, Bill was working and Louie was greeted by Mary and Johnny. They were glad to see him and, while they were all eating, the two discussed the benefits of life in California. Louie could not help noticing how beautiful Mary had become and how she had a relaxed, carefree way about her. He thought that Hollywood had really made a change in this small-town girl from upstate New York. Mary took him around the neighborhood and introduced him to the local cab-drivers who all liked her very much and who had a stand around the corner on Santa Monica Boulevard.

When Bill returned home later that evening, he inquired about Louie's plans, and he made it clear that his brother could only stay until things were safe for him to return to Johnstown. Johnny was still doing day work and had been out for a few hours. Upon his return, he informed Louie about the gambling ship which was anchored three miles off the beach of Santa Monica. A spark lit up in Louie's eye, and for the first time since his arrival, he showed a keen interest in some of the information about California. He remembered a Hollywood movie with Cary Grant which involved a similar gambling ship. Now he was feeling much more relaxed and thinking about how he, Louie, was going to get there.

Poor Bill found himself supporting three others besides himself since Johnny and Louie would hardly ever work once the gambling ship was discovered. He did not mind taking care of his wife, but these two other reprobates were something else. Another worry for Bill was his brother's being constantly around Mary. When it came to the opposite sex, he knew that Louie had no scruples whatsoever and had been tempted to approach Mary but, in consideration for his brother and the anger which would come from his parents, Don Guglielmo and Donida should he further do anything adulterous, he kept his distance. All the years that his parents were alive, Louie would never talk back to them or be disrespectful. He understood the rule of "Do not bite the hand that feeds you," and they fed him for a very long time.

Life seemed to be moving along for the four transplants from New York. Bill was enjoying a growing reputation as a good worker and a very dependable boss. Mary was living like a movie star getting a lot of attention from all sorts of people, and she was adapting to the Californian life-style as if born to it. Johnny and Louie were indulging in exactly what they had enjoyed when they lived in Johnstown. New surroundings! Same life!

One night, a shocking incident put a fright into Mary, Louie and Johnny. After a day on the gambling ship, Louie and Johnny returned home to find Bill on the couch all bandaged up and in a very rough shape. Bill had started to manifest the traits that would eventually define him and his manner as a middle-manager. He exercised these traits on the Mexicans who worked under him at the wool pullery and he found that they did not take to his bossy ways. As he was leaving the plant that night, four Mexicans were waiting for him in the shadows, jumped him, and gave him a terrible beating. Bill was in such rough shape that he did not go into work the next morning and Johnny took the car and drove down Figueroa to Soto and into the town of Vernon. When Johnny approached the plant, he did not even stop the car and drove it right into the office He climbed out and demanded that the Mexicans, who had beaten up Bill, should come out and face him. There were no takers to Johnny's offer and he returned to Hollywood. Bill never did learn a lesson from this or similar incidents. All through his life, he would carry on in his own way, pushing workers to the edge and not considering the possible consequences. He did, however, as years went by, become a very well loved, highly respected, dynamic and powerful figure who always cared for and provided for those who worked for him.

What next? Bill was beginning to wonder who would be the next visitor heading to the little bungalow in the West. He would find out in a few days. During the last six months, Don Guglielmo had been receiving intimate letters from his son, Bill, in California who had been looking for forgiveness and redemption for what he thought was complete lack of honoring his father's expectations of him. In these letters, Bill Jr. was attempting to reassure his father that he was going to make something out of his life and carve out a future for himself and for his family. The old man was touched by the letters and was becoming an old man indeed.

It was approximately twenty-eight years since Guglielmo (William) Fioravanti had landed at Ellis Island and prepared to find life in the New World. He was fifty-four years old and, in all the years that he had lived in America, he had never really had a vacation or seen much of the country that he loved so much. He made a decision to attempt the trip to California to see his sons and his daughter-in-law.

Bill Sr.'s family in Johnstown knew that a bus trip would be trying and exhausting for this man who was getting on in life. Michael Mazzaro came up with a solution which would make the family reassured of Bill's safety and health. It would be best for him to travel by train. In earlier times train travel would have been prohibitive as far as price was concerned, but just as the world was progressing, so was the United States In 1937, the railroad companies had introduced trains which were increasingly faster and more efficient. The Santa Fe Line had completed the stream-lined train called El Capitan. This was made of highly polished stainless steel and the engine was designed from a new advanced form of engineering. The Twentieth Century Limited was the east's answer to the Santa Fe 's modern train of coach-equipped seating with reclining seats so that one could sleep very comfortably. Both of these train lines had dining cars and lounges so that the traveler could relax and enjoy the trip and beauty of America's changing landscape The fare was reasonable and not much more expensive than the cost of bus travel.

Plans were settled and Don Guglielmo began preparations to leave for California. He knew, despite the country's woes, all would be well at his home of 22, Cayadutta Street since his daughters Mary and Josie and Michael Mazzaro were all bringing in income for the family. In order not to disrupt the winter festivities, he decided to leave for California in March of 1939. There was a certain itinerary that Don Guglielmo had in mind for when he arrived in Hollywood, and it was one that none of his children, who were presently in California, would have even remotely considered. First, he would take in all the landscape and cities on his trip out west. Once in Hollywood, he planned to visit all the motion-picture-studios and he knew just how he would gain entrance to them without causing a stir.

By now, Louie was tiring of California and feeling very homesick, and news that his father was planning to visit did not make him happy. After all, nothing had changed with him. He was still gambling, chasing women and, once again, was out of a job. He feared his father's fury and, rather than face the inevitable tongue-lashing, decided to leave California before his father's arrival.

March weather in Upstate New York is usually wet, cold and damp and the day when Don Guglielmo prepared to board the Twentieth Century Limited, bound for Chicago, was no different. Darkness was just beginning to envelop the landscape and it would turn out to be a trip in total darkness all the way to the Windy City. Mike and Mary waved good-bye as the train pulled out of the Fonda Station. Bill Sr.'s new adventure had now begun.

Bill Sr. slept most of the way to Chicago and was awakened a few miles from LaSalle Street Station, which was the Limited's final destination. Upon the train's arrival, the passengers were given directions for the next part of their trips. He detrained and made his way to Dearborn Station which was only a few blocks away. There he would board the relatively new El Capitan train with its reclining chairs which gave rest to the weary travelers. It was not long before the train left the station and was chugging and smoking as it made its way westward.

Simultaneously, in Los Angeles, Louie was boarding a Greyhound bus which was bound for Joplin, Missouri. He had not wanted to face his father and was truly missing his old life back in Johnstown. His brother Bill Jr., had put together all the money that he could muster to buy a ticket for him, but the afforded fare would only take him as far as Joplin. Bill Jr. also gave him as much spending money as he could spare. Louie figured that, if he could get out of the Southwest, he could eventually hitch rides for the rest of the way to New York. As it turned out, Louie would have the time of his life making the rest of the journey back to Johnstown. By the time he reached Joplin, Missouri, he had spent and gambled all the spare money and, for the rest of the trip, he would have to fend for himself.

Oddly enough, somewhere along the way, Bill Sr.'s train and Louie's bus would pass each other and this was without either one being aware of it. The two arrivals could have not been more different. Louie would get home wearing women's stockings, someone's short pants, a filthy cap and shoes with no soles. His body was covered with black soot and filth from hopping freight cars from rail yard to rail yard. He had had to beg for food and clothing. This was Louie's first introduction to humility which would be a lesson that he would never forget. When he tried to enter the house at 22, Cayadutta Street, he was confronted by Donida, his mother, who did not recognize him and started to scream out and beg for the police. Louie finally calmed her down and made her realize that he was her son. From this, Donida cried for hours and finally asked if Louie knew that his father was on his way to California. He replied that he knew and asked if he could clean-up and take a bath. While submerged in the tub, Louie contemplated his eventual confrontation with the "boxer" and gave into the inevitability that he would have to take a beating. He finally took that beating and, afterwards, as he was in a lot of pain, was content in the knowledge that he was home safe and sound. It would be only one more time that Louie would leave home again and that was to be when "Uncle Sam" sent him the notice: "We Want You" Unfortunately, this was to be another distasteful experience.

Don Guglielmo's train slowed down as it moved into La Grande Station in Los Angeles. For the senior gentleman from Johnstown, it had been a marvelous trip. He had seen the wonders of the great Mid-West and the beauty of the South-West and was contented and very excited when he prepared to de-train. A strange coincidence was preparing to come to fruition just as it had been when he had arrived at the old Grand Central Station back in 1910. A month after Don Guglielmo's arrival at La Grande Station, it was torn down and a new one was about to be constructed. This would be called the Los Angeles Union Passenger Terminal and opened its doors on May 7, 1939. Up to the present day, it would remain the primary station for all trains arriving from the East. Eventually, it was to be known simply as Union Station and again, a Hollywood movie called "Union Station" was to take its name.

As he searched for his sons and his daughter-in-law, Don Guglielmo finally spotted Mary and Johnny, but, where were Louie and Bill Jr.? A thin man, dressed in a white linen suit, a white shirt, a black tie, white buck-skin shoes and a pencil moustache that he did not recognize, approached him. It was a shock to see his son, Bill Jr. materialize in front of his very eyes. The two men greeted each other with much affection and joy. Another surprise for Don Guglielmo was Mary, whom he kissed and who he could see had blossomed into a beautiful girl. He asked as to Louie's whereabouts and was told that he had just left for Johnstown, homesick and miserable. Don Guglielmo took the news in his stride, and they all left for Bill and Mary's bungalow on Spaulding Avenue.

As the 1931 Buick moved along from the train station to Spaulding Avenue, Don Guglielmo could not help but notice the similarity between the terrain of Sicily and that of Southern California. The hills were brown and burned from the sun and the palm trees were reminiscent of tropical climes. He also noticed the width of the roads and how beautifully they had been laid down, and he enjoyed the warm weather and the light cool breeze that tempered the air. To him, this truly was a paradise and, for the short time he would spend in this paradise, he would submerge himself as if in an endless, euphoric pool.

By his first glance at the bungalow on Spaulding Avenue, Don Guglielmo was amazed at the Spanish design and of the house's modern appearance. Since home builders in Southern California always had a tendency to overbuild and develop, the houses there were very affordable to either rent or purchase. This overbuilding would continue in California until the late 1960's.

Upon entering the house, the smell of fresh sauce simmering on the stove filled the air, and Don Guglielmo finally felt at ease for the first time in the last four days. He was shown to his room which had been Johnny's, but who now would sleep on the couch for the duration of the stay. As was his way, when Don Guglielmo had unpacked and cleaned up, he made a close examination of the interior of the bungalow and he was duly impressed. As they all sat down to eat, Mary served spaghetti and the meat-balls which she had made. Don

Guglielmo was enjoying the cooking and commented as to how Mary had progressed as a cook and as a home-maker. Her meat-balls would indeed become a sort of trade-mark for her in later years as, all through her life, her children, their friends, and eventually her grandchildren would all come searching for them.

During the meal, Bill Sr. listened as Bill Jr. told him of his job, his plans for the future, and the general benefits of living and working in Southern California. The father could not help noticing how his son's attitude had changed.   He had developed a work ethic and this would carry him through the rest of his life. There was another change which the old man noticed in his son. He had the leadership qualities which were developing at a rapid rate and ones which Don Guglielmo himself did not possess. He was elated to find them in Bill Jr. The new confidence which he had found in his son, together with the outgoing signs that Mary now exhibited, had already made his trip out west worthwhile.

After the meal which included wine and pastries, Don Guglielmo retired to his room and slept soundly until morning. He awoke to find that Bill Jr. had already left for work but had promised that he would take his father to his place of employment and introduce him to Mr. Grossman and show him around the plant. However, in the meantime, Johnny and Mary would be his guides around Hollywood and Los Angeles. When Don Guglielmo first approached the subject of entering the big motion studios, Mary and Johnny told him that it would be impossible for him to gain entrance. Once again, the old man would show the ingenuity that had helped him to survive all these years in America. He went into his room and came out with a small bundle inside of which were the tools of the cobbler's trade. He knew that all of the major studios employed cobblers to design and fit all the stars and actors with shoes appropriate for the particular production being shot at the time.

Armed with his bundle and the confidence that he would realize his goal Don Guglielmo, Johnny, and his daughter-in-law set off for 20th Century Fox's Studios as they were in the closest proximity to Spaulding Avenue. Upon their arrival at the entrance to Fox Studios on Pico Boulevard, Johnny parked the car and the three New York natives approached the guard at the gate. Johnny and Mary would not be admitted, but as soon as Don Guglielmo opened his bundle and exhibited his cobbler's tools, the guard made a 'phone call and everything opened up for him.

As Don Guglielmo passed through the gate, he was astonished by the vastness of what is called a studio lot. Ancient buildings, winding alleys and cobblestone roads were all confronting him as he made his way towards the building that housed the shoe-makers who produced all the shoes and boots that the actors wore during the making of their movies. As a very handsome man approached Bill Sr., he was asked for directions to his destination. The man, who happened to be the movie star, Robert Montgomery, and who was gracious and elegant, was very helpful and pointed him in the right direction. Bill Sr. was impressed.

At last, he entered the work-shop of the shoe and boot-makers and it was a joy to behold. The shoe-makers were mostly Italians and Sicilians who had come directly from their own countries. They welcomed Bill into their domain and proceeded to show him and explain all the nuances that were involved in making shoes for the stars. For Bill, the most impressive part of the experience was being introduced to the latest, modern equipment that he had ever seen. This was a far distance from what he had known in his early days as a cobbler. He thought to himself that, when he returned home, he would have many things to tell his friend, Michael Mazzaro, who had been a shoe designer for so many years before he arrived in Johnstown.

Don Guglielmo was reflecting on all that he had seen and in the manner in which he had been accepted by the men who made up the work-force that covered the actors' feet, which would ultimately tread their way through thousands of movies. He was amazed at the enormous sound stages and their ability to house what seemed to be complete towns and cities. His only regret was that he had not seen any locations for westerns. Unfortunately, these lots were in the back of the studios where there was open land and room for horses and cattle and for other miscellaneous items associated with westerns. All that Don Guglielmo had seen at Fox Studios would many years later be sold to developers who would create a Mecca in the City of Hollywood which would eventually be known as Century City.

Johnny and Mary later took Don Guglielmo to two more studios which were Paramount and M.G.M., and the latter impressed him the most. There he not only met the men who made and designed the boots and shoes, but he was exposed to the most colorful of all the studios. Here the great musicals were produced and boasted such stars as Jeanette MacDonald, Nelson Eddy, Gene Kelly, Greer Garson, and many others. The actors, who were in the studio "streets", were dressed in costumes that exuded glamour and excitement. It was like a flood of bright and sparkling light that filled the air. What a world was this of make-believe and fantasy! Don Guglielmo felt he would explode if he were exposed to much more. Nevertheless, before he left Hollywood, he would in person see Joan Crawford and Franchot Tone, her husband at the time, and even the grand old gal, May Robson. He would visit the homes of Marion Davis, Loretta Young and the movies' Tarzan, Johnny Weissmuller.

For this elderly gentleman, all that was now left for him was to visit his son's workplace and meet Henry Grossman, a man he had heard so much about in the last year. Bill Jr. finally took his father to the wool pullery to meet Henry and, of course, Don Guglielmo was impressed. This was not surprising since he had had hopes that his son, Bill Jr., would have become a lawyer. The fact that Henry could give up law for a job in the wool business was what bothered the old man the most. As the Depression had forced many old law firms to close and go into bankruptcy, this was becoming a common occurrence in the legal field, and Don Guglielmo could never seem to understand this, but he could realize that his own son had seemed to find his way. This created warmth within him and he felt that he would later be happy to report to Michael Mazzaro that Bill Jr. would know a good future.

With only a few days left in California before he would board the train to return to the East, Don Guglielmo enjoyed the remaining time relaxing and spending days with his daughter-in-law and nights with his son. Finally, the day of departure arrived and he boarded the El Capitan bound for Chicago and expressed his sadness in leaving behind what appeared to be an almost perfect world and in bidding good-bye to two people whom he loved very much. There were many tears and much sobbing as Mary and Bill Jr. watched the train pull-out of La Grande Station. It was if they felt that they would never see each other again. It seems so strange how moments can stimulate the imagination and how one can then find out that all was illusion.

Only a few weeks after Don Guglielmo had left California, Mary discovered that she was pregnant, and this event changed everyone's life forever. She could not deal with the thought of having a child in such a faraway place without the support of family around her. She explained to Bill Jr. that she would like to go home and he was not receptive to her suggestion, but she was adamant and determined. In early June, Mary left by bus to travel back to Johnstown, and this left Bill alone again with many decisions to finalize. It was because of her life-long fear of riding in trains that she had gone by bus.

There would have to be an encounter with Henry Grossman since it was only right that he be given notice if Bill Jr. was to leave his position and return to Johnstown. Henry tried to persuade him to give Mary time after which, perhaps, she might alter her mind and return. Bill knew that this would never happen but was convinced by Henry to stay on until late October in the hope that something would change. However, as Bill suspected, nothing changed with Mary and, in late October, Bill and Johnny loaded up the Buick and set forth on a trip into the past.

Bill and Mary never did recapture the wonderful life which they had had in California. She reverted to the provincial woman that she had been before she went out West, and she stayed that way forever. Bill Jr., although he became very successful in the workplace, found it extremely hard to exist in a world he never made and he would suffer psychological problems throughout his life. Their ending was not perfect, but they endured. It was 1939.

Epilogue

The journey of Guglielmo (William) Fioravanti and the events which shaped and motivated his life were peculiarly his, but he was not the only Sicilian who had ventured forth from poverty and desperation to seek a new life in a colonial village called Johnstown.

Many Sicilian immigrants found their way here: the Raneri's, Russo's, Lizio's, the Ruggeri families, the Alfano and Brunetto families, the Rizio's, the Turrisi, Taddune, Fugazzatto, Caraco, Mazzaro, Piccione and Melita families, the Greco's, Entelissano, Minardo, Precopio, Pagano, Pelosi, Izzano, Papa, Liccardi, Genovese, and many more families. These Sicilians, who also risked their lives like my grandfather, have a story to tell, but that belongs to them.

Don Guglielmo Fioravanti passed in 1963 and would live to see the high-school graduations of all his five grandchildren and of his brother, Giuseppe Andreana's grandchildren. He would not live to see any of his grandchildren graduate from college. All through his life, the simple things of learning, music, and morality were what meant most to him. His wife, Donida, predeceased him in 1962.

Don Guglielmo's grand friend, Michael Mazzaro, died in 1948. He had lived long enough to help rear Bill Jr., Constantino, and Mary and Josie, and he continued his influence on the lives of three of Bill Jr.'s children during their formative years. He had been an impact persona in the Fioravanti family, and he stamped his mark on them all.

Don Guglielmo's last big adventure was in 1949 when he and Mary, his first-born child, set sail for a final trip to his homeland of Sicily. There he would visit old haunts and go to see Michael Mazzaro's sisters in the town of Avella. His daughter, Mary, would find herself a husband.

In his final days, all he could say was that he was tired and moved on.

About the Author

William V. Fioravanti was born and reared in the Colonial town of Johnstown , New York. He caught the tail end of the bigotry and hatred that had haunted his father and grandfather.

The author eventually graduated from Syracuse University where he had studied intensely in Theatre, Literature, and Political Science and History.

After many years in the world of business he returned to writing plays and the short book about his grandfather. It is his wish that anyone who reads his work "A Sicilian's Journey" will catch a glimpse of the immigrant experience from a different point of view.

Made in United States
Orlando, FL
06 January 2022

12988954R00081